Cloud Computing
with
Google Chrome

George Root

Cloud Computing with Google Chrome

by George Root

March 2013: First Edition

A Kindle version of this book is available from the Kindle Store.
Search for the title "Cloud Computing with Google Chrome"

ISBN-13: 978-1483902258
ISBN-10: 1483902250

Table of Contents

Preface

About the Author

Hi, my name is **George Root**.

I graduated with an MSEE degree from Caltech back in the dark ages before there were personal computers. I began my career in the aerospace industry starting with the big mainframe computers from Univac, IBM, and DEC. During my career I have written thousands of pages of technical documentation. But writing this book on Chrome has been my most enjoyable writing project.

In 1985 I saw a demonstration of a new type of computer called a "Macintosh". It immediately struck me that this was the way computers were supposed to work. I bought a Mac and ever since then I have been a fan of, some might say fanatic about, Apple computers.

Then one day, not long ago, a friend asked me what I knew about Chrome computers. I knew that there was a web browser from Google called Chrome, but I didn't know there was also a Chrome Operating System and that computers were being built to run that OS. I started reading about Chrome and was once again struck by the thought "this is the way computers are supposed to work".

I bought a Samsung Chromebook and began trying to figure out how to use it. I found that many things about Chrome are different from the way my Mac and other personal computers work. This book summarizes what I have learned.

I hope you find this book useful and join me in my admiration for the work that Google has put into their "next big thing". If you do find this book useful, I would appreciate it if you would stop by the Amazon Book Store and give it a good review. Thanks!

I am not affiliated in any way with Google except as a customer.

You can send me feedback about this book at:

ChromeBookFeedback@gmail.com

Why Did I Write this Book?

To tell the truth I didn't set out to write a book about Chrome. I really wanted to buy one. I had just bought my first Chromebook computer and I wanted a book to tell me how to set up and use all of the nifty new features of Chrome. Chrome cloud computing is different in several ways from using an "ordinary" personal computer and I needed a guide to help me through the learning process. Perhaps you feel the same way.

Unable to find a book that answered all of my questions, I ended up researching hundreds of Google Chrome Support web pages. At the same time I was experimenting with my ChromeBook and trying to put into practice what I was learning. Some of these experiments were less than successful. I started taking notes to summarize what I had learned both from my reading as well as from my hands-on experience.

It occurred to me that I might not be the only one who needed a little help getting to know Chrome and that an up-to-date Chrome book might be useful to other people like me. Even if you have been using Chrome for a while, you may not be familiar with the latest Chrome features like "2-Step Verification" or "Application Specific Passwords" and you will also find useful information in this book.

Google Chrome is a moving target - it is constantly evolving and improving. New features are added. Old features are updated. The contents of this book are up to date as of March 2013, and Chrome version 26 (beta), but some things may be different by the time you read this. Hopefully those differences will be small.

What You Will Find in this Book

At last count, Google had about 50 different apps and services and no single book can cover all of them. The purpose of this book is primarily to explain setting up your Google Accounts and working with the Chrome Browser and Operating System.

Specifically I will discuss those apps closely associated with the Chrome Operating System:

- Chrome Browser and Chrome Computers
- Gmail
- Google Drive
- Google Docs
- Google Cloud Print

I will not cover what might be called the Google "Social" apps:

- Google Talk
- Google Voice
- Google Play
- Google+
- YouTube
- Picasa

Many of you will already be familiar with these social apps since they are not specific to the Chrome web browser.

I have tried to organize this book more or less in the same order you would need the information if you were starting out with a new ChromeBook. I will, as much as possible, cover both the Chrome Browser you may already have installed on your current personal computer, and the Chrome Operating System that powers Chrome Devices like ChromeBooks.

1 - What is Google Chrome?

1.1 - Google Chrome is "The Next Big Thing"

To many people Google is the search engine that we all use to find stuff on the web. But in the background, Google, the company, has been inventing "The Next Big Thing". And that next big thing is Chrome. Chrome is going to revolutionize the way computing is done in the future. And you can experience that future right now. This book is going to tell you how.

Chrome is actually two different things. You may know Chrome as a web browser like Safari on the Mac or FireFox on PCs. The Chrome web browser lets you experience the full glory of Chrome at no cost and using the computer you already own. The Chrome browser runs on every kind of computer and device: Macs, PCs, iPads, Android phones, etc.

But Chrome is much more than a simple web browser. It is also an operating system, Chrome OS, just like Windows on a PC or OS X on a Mac. There is a wealth of applications (apps) that run on the Chrome OS. But these apps, for the most part, don't reside on your personal computer. The revolutionary aspect of Chrome is that most of the apps reside on Google servers somewhere in the "cloud". Your documents aren't stored on your personal computer either, but on the Google cloud servers. There are many advantages to this approach which I will discuss shortly. Perhaps the most "revolutionary" aspect of Chrome is that for the most part, everything is free!

But first,

1.2 - What Devices Does Chrome Run On?

Chrome, the **web browser**, runs on your present personal computer. And the Chrome browser window looks and acts very much like Chrome OS running on a dedicated computer. So, you can see what the Chrome OS looks and feels like using the computer you already own.

Chrome OS, the **operating system**, runs on a new breed of computers called ChromeBooks (laptops) or ChromeBoxes (desktops). Basically these are Linux computers designed to run the Chrome OS. When you launch the Chrome OS on one of these Chrome Devices, the window that opens looks very much like the Chrome browser window on your personal computer.

This is an exciting time in the world of Chrome Devices. At the time I'm writing this, the Samsung ChromeBook has been the best selling computer on Amazon for 125 straight days, and the variety of Chrome Devices is expanding daily. There are currently Chrome Devices available from: Acer, HP, Lenovo, Samsung, and now from Google itself. Here is a sampling of what's available now, arranged in order of price:

- Acer C7 ChromeBook: $200
- Samsung ChromeBook: $250 (WiFi only) or $330 (WiFi + 3G Cellular Data)
- Samsung ChromeBox: $330
- HP Pavilion 14 ChromeBook: $330
- Lenovo Thinkpad ChromeBook: $430
- Samsung ChromeBook Series 5: $450 (WiFi only) or $550 (WiFi+3G Cellular)
- Google "Pixel": $1300 (WiFi only) or $1500 (WiFi + LTE Cellular Data)

No, that's not a typo. The Google Pixel costs $1000 more than its ChromeBook competitors. This has led some to speculate that the true target is not other ChromeBook makers, but Apple's MacBook Pro. To be fair, the price of the Google Pixel does include 2 years of 1TB storage on Google servers (normally $1200) and the price of the LTE model includes 2 years of "free" cell data (100 MB/month).

If you are interested in buying a Chrome Device be sure to check out the specs on all the available devices. There are a lot of differences between them in addition to price. Some have disk drives and some have solid-state drives (SSD). By the time you read this, there will probably be even more Chrome Devices to choose from.

So, you might ask: "If I can run the Chrome browser on my current personal computer, why would I want to buy a ChromeBook?"

For one thing, ChromeBooks are very inexpensive. The Samsung ChromeBook costs $250 and it is a credible substitute for the Apple MacBook Air at $1000 to $1500. So, if you travel a lot, as I do, it makes more sense to carry around my $250 ChromeBook rather than a $1500 MacBook Air. But, the thing that makes ChromeBooks really inexpensive is that most of the apps are free.

Perhaps the most important difference between Chrome Devices and Windows PCs, and to a lesser extent Macs, is security. If you lose your Windows or Mac laptop, you lose everything that was stored on it - think company secrets. If you lose your ChromeBook, you lose nothing, except the $250 it will cost to replace it. There is almost nothing stored on the ChromeBook. Everything will still be there waiting for you on the Google servers the next time you sign-in.

1.3 - Why Should You Use Chrome?

There are a myriad of advantages that Chrome has over regular personal computers. Here are just a few:

1.3.1 - Inexpensive hardware and software

Chrome Devices have limited onboard memory and don't need a lot of CPU horsepower since all of the heavy lifting is done on and by Google, or other website, servers. So the local hardware is relatively simple and inexpensive. And, as I mentioned above, most of the apps are free. Storage on Google servers is also free (for the first 5GB).

1.3.2 - Security

Perhaps the biggest advantage of Chrome is security.

Almost all Chrome software resides on Google servers so it is very difficult to infect your local Chrome Device. Local apps are heavily sandboxed limiting their ability to interact with any other app's data. If Google detects a weakness in Chrome, it gets patched quickly, and your version of Chrome gets patched automatically at the same time. You don't have to do anything. That phrase "You don't have to do anything" is perhaps the biggest security advantage of Chrome. Google takes care of everything.

Everything that gets transmitted between your Chrome Device and the Google servers, as well as all your synced data that is stored on the Google servers, is (optionally) encrypted. And backed up. Automatically.

Google has also taken the next step in password protection. Google calls it "2-Step Verification". The idea is that your Chrome Account password is just a single verification factor. Your password is something that you know (hopefully). Google adds something that you own - your cell phone - as a second factor needed in order to sign-in to your Chrome Account. Two-Step Verification can still work if you don't own a cell phone or if your cell phone gets lost or stolen. I will explain the details of how all this works in Section 3.3.2.

Although Chrome is, when compared to any other OS available today, very, very secure, that doesn't mean that it is entirely secure. In fact, when Google released Chrome version 25 recently, it patched 22 security flaws that had been discovered since the version 24 release. But that just illustrates why Chrome is so secure. Google pays cash prizes to anyone who finds a flaw in Chrome. They paid out about $25,000 to the people who discovered the flaws that were patched in version 25.

1.3.3- Always in Sync

When you create a Chrome document - a word processing document, a spreadsheet, a slide presentation, or any of the other document types that Chrome provides - that document gets stored on Google servers. As you work on your document, Chrome automatically saves it to the Google servers every few seconds. This means that you can sign-in to your Chrome Account from any computer and you will see exactly the same stuff that was there when you last signed-out even if that was on a different computer. In fact all of your Chrome account information is stored on Google servers so that you can sign-in from any computer and everything you see will look just like it did when you last left it. All of your apps, settings, contacts, email messages, calendar events, and documents will be there. All in sync - all automatically.

This is really quite remarkable. One night I added two new extensions to my Chromebook. The next morning I fired up the Chrome Browser on my Mac and lo-and-behold, there were the two new extensions, already installed on my Mac. Once again, I didn't have to do anything. Google keeps all of your Chrome Browsers and Chrome Devices in sync - always.

In some cases a local copy of a document is retained on your Chrome Device so that you can work on it even if you don't have Internet access. This document will be sent back to the Google servers as soon as your Internet access is re-established.

1.3.4 - No IT Department Needed

Businesses love Chrome because it eliminates the need for a big IT (Information Technology) department. Google handles all the IT chores keeping apps and the Chrome OS itself up to date on all Chrome devices. If a security flaw is discovered in Chrome, Google fixes it and that fixes it on all Chrome devices automatically.

1.3.5 - Easy Collaboration

For business users the "always in sync" aspect of Chrome makes collaboration on a project easy. When you create a Chrome document, you can grant access to that document to other Chrome users. Several people can be working on a single document at the same time. Changes made by one person will be (almost) instantly visible to the other users. Part of the Chrome automatic saving feature is that it also provides version memory. You can revert back to a previous version if necessary.

1.4 - Sometimes Chrome Terminology Can Be a Bit Confusing

Although Chrome is a fantastic new technology, the terminology that Google has chosen to describe it is, at times, confusing. I'll try to make sense of it here:

1.4.1 - "Chrome" vs "Chrome OS"

As I pointed out above, "Chrome" actually refers to two different, but similar, things.

One "Chrome" is a **web browser** that can be downloaded free and installed on your present personal computer or smart phone. Get this "Chrome" at:

https://www.google.com/intl/en/chrome/browser/

You can try out Chrome using this free browser without investing any money.

The Chrome **operating system** - called "Chrome OS" - runs on special computers designed for just that one purpose. Only with these purpose-built computers are the full features of Chrome available. This is particularly true of the security features.

The Chrome Browser differs from the Chrome OS running on a Chrome Device in two important ways:

1) The Chrome Browser does not replace the operating system that runs your present personal computer. The Chrome Browser is just an app that runs on your personal computer like any other

app. All of the security issues and vulnerabilities of your personal computer still exist. So, you still need to install and update your anti-virus software as usual.

In contrast, the Chrome OS running on a Chrome Device is very secure and, at this time, no anti-virus software is needed.

2) The Chrome OS is the operating system that runs your Chrome Device. You can have multiple user accounts on a Chrome Device just as with any other personal computer. To switch users, you will sign-out of the current user account and then sign-in to a different account. Only one account at a time.

In contrast, within the Chrome Browser running on your personal computer you can have multiple user accounts open at the same time. Each user will appear in its own window and switching between them is as simple as switching browser windows. Refer to Section 3.5, which discusses this in more detail.

1.4.2 - Google "Docs" vs "Google Docs"

Are you confused yet? Sometimes Google Docs refers to a subset of all the apps available for Chrome. Specifically, the Chrome word processor app, the spreadsheet app, and the slide presentation app are referred to collectively as "Google Docs". You will recognize these as being similar to the Microsoft Office suite of apps: Word, Excel, and PowerPoint or, if you're a Mac user: Pages, Numbers, and Keynote. Chrome provides a free replacement for each of these Office apps.

Unfortunately, Google has also chosen to name their word processor app "Docs". The spreadsheet app is named "Sheets", and the slide presentation app is named "Slides". So, we are left with the unfortunate situation where "Docs" sometimes refers to the word processor, and sometimes it refers to the entire suite of Office-like apps.

In this book I will use quotes to distinguish between these two "Docs". I will use "Google Docs" - quotes around both words - to refer to the suite of apps and Google "Docs" - quotes around the word Docs only - to refer to the word processing app. Google is replacing the use of "Docs" with "Documents" to refer to the word processing app, so this confusion may disappear by the time you read this.

1.4.3 - "Apps" vs "Extensions"

Chrome can run hundreds of different software programs. Some are built into Chrome and the others can be purchased - mostly free - from the Chrome Webstore (see Section 2.7). You will find three categories of stuff on the Chrome Webstore: "Apps", "Extensions", and "Themes". What the heck is the difference between an "App" and an "Extension" and a "Theme"?

1.4.3.1 Apps:

The classical Chrome "app", now called a "Hosted App", is really just a link to a website hidden behind the icon you see and click on when you want to launch the app. "NetFlix" and "Pandora Radio" are examples of this type of web app. All of the processing is done by the website. Basically nothing gets installed on your device running Chrome except the link to the website. In addition, the developer of a Hosted App must verify that they own the website that their app runs on. For these reasons Hosted Apps are very safe. They cannot interact with your local hardware. They cannot install software on your device running Chrome.

There is a second type of "app" being introduced into the Chrome world. This type is called a "Packaged App". Packaged Apps are very like conventional apps that get installed on Windows and Mac computers. All of the code is installed locally. Packaged Apps can run without an Internet connection and can provide functionality not possible with Hosted Apps. Packaged Apps can also run outside the Chrome Browser, appearing in their own separate window.

1.4.3.2 Extensions:

A Chrome "extension" is software installed on your computer running the Chrome Browser. It "extends", that is, it adds functionality to the Chrome Browser. Because "extensions" are actually installed on your device, they pose more risk than "apps" and thus require more thought than when installing apps. You might, for example, consider how many users have installed this extension before you. You might also want to read any reviews before deciding whether or not to install the extension.

1.4.3.3 - Themes:

Themes change the way the Chrome browser looks but they do not affect its functionality. If you get bored with how your Chrome browser looks, you might like to try a different Theme.

1.5 - Concerns About Using Chrome

There are two primary concerns about using Chrome:

1.5.1 What Happens If I Don't Have an Internet Connection?

Without an Internet connection Chrome loses much, but not all of its functionality. Clearly, you cannot listen to Pandora Radio nor stream YouTube videos without the Internet. But Google is working to enable some of its apps to function without an Internet connection. Google "Docs", the word processor, can create, display, and edit word processing Docs while offline. These Docs will be automatically uploaded to the Google servers when a connection is re-established. Google "Sheets", the spreadsheet app, can display sheets offline, but cannot edit them while offline (yet). Eventually all of the Chrome "business apps": Docs, Sheets, and Slides, will be operational offline.

"**Gmail Offline**", an app available in the Chrome WebStore, allows you to read and compose email messages while offline.

In addition, Google is introducing "Packaged Apps" that developers can create and which can function without the Internet.

The fact is that most of what typical users do on their current personal computers such as: email, web browsing, shopping, FaceBook, YouTube, Skype, etc, all require an Internet connection to function. In this respect Chrome is no different than any other personal computer.

1.5.2 What About Data Security? Is My Data Safe on Google Servers?

The short answer is that your data is probably safer on Google servers than it is on your current personal computer. All of your synced data stored on Google servers is (optionally) encrypted. All communication between your Chrome device and Google is encrypted. Everything on the Google servers gets backed up regularly. Access to your data is protected by 2-Step Verification. In all these respects your data with Google is safer than it would be on your own computer.

The real concern is not that some hacker will somehow gain access to your information, but rather that Google will. There is no doubt that Google uses your information for its own purposes - mainly to sell advertising. However, Google clearly states what information it collects about you and why it does that. Google has recently announced that it will no longer provide user information to law enforcement agencies without a probable cause warrant issued by a court.

Briefly, here is the type of information Google collects:
The information you supply when you sign up for a Google Account or a Google Profile: your name, email address, telephone number, age, and photo. Information about the hardware you are using such as the type of computer you are using, the OS you are using, and your IP address. Search queries you submit to the Google search engine. Crash reports including hardware and browser information. Telephone information including your phone number, and the number you are calling, the date, time, and duration of the call. Google will place cookies on your computer that will identify your browser and Google account. If you are using Google Maps on a mobile device Google will collect information about your location and nearby WiFi access points.

All of this is explained in the Google Privacy Policy which you can read here:

http://www.google.com/policies/privacy/

You must agree to all of this in order to set up a Google Account.

2 - Getting Familiar with Your Chrome Device

Once you get your Chrome Device up and running, you can always get Help by going to:

https://support.google.com/chrome/

2.1 - The Chrome Keyboard & Touchpad

2.1.1 - Chrome Keyboard:

Probably the first thing you will notice when you open your ChromeBook for the first time is that the keyboard looks a little different from what you are used to. For one thing there's no "Caps Lock" key. What should be the Caps Lock key has a "?" symbol on it. Clicking on this key is equivalent to clicking on the "waffle icon" in the Launcher Bar. As explained in Section 2.4 this opens a menu of all the apps installed on your Chrome Device including a search box where you can initiate a web search.

If you really want a caps-lock key, hold down the "alt" key while hitting the "?" key. This turns caps-lock on. To turn caps-lock back off, hold down "alt" and hit "?"again.

The other difference with the Chrome keyboard is that the top row of keys - what would be the row of function keys on a PC - now have different functions.

Figure 2.1 - The Top Row of the Chrome Keyboard

The functions of these keys, going from left to right, are as follows:

- The "left arrow" key goes to the previous browser page (F1)
- The "right arrow" key goes to the next browser page (F2)
- The "circular arrow" key reloads the current browser page (F3)
- The "rectangle with two corners marked" key maximizes the browser window (F4)
- The "stack of cards" key near the middle goes to the next browser window (F5). This key has an even more important function - particularly if you're writing a book about Chrome. Holding down

the "ctrl" key and tapping on this key (F5) takes a screen shot of the entire current Chrome screen. Holding down the "ctrl" and "shift" keys while tapping this key (F5) changes the cursor into a little set of crosshairs. Use the mouse or touchpad to drag this cursor so that it outlines a rectangular area of the screen and a screenshot of that area will be taken. These screenshots get stored in the "Downloads" folder inside the "Files" folder.

• The "small starburst" key lowers screen brightness (F6)

• The "big starburst" key increases screen brightness (F7)

• The "speaker with a line through it" key mutes sound (F8)

• The "small speaker" key lowers sound level (F9)

• The "big speaker" key increases sound level (F10)

If you're using a Chrome Box, you have to supply your own keyboard so it will probably look like a standard PC keyboard but the keys still function as they do with a ChromeBook. The "F#" in each key description above shows you which function key to press.

2.1.2 - Chrome Keyboard Shortcuts:

There are many keyboard shortcuts that you can use on a Chrome Device. You can see a full list by typing Ctrl+Alt+?. Here are a few of my favorites:

All the "Standard" Keyboard Shortcuts Work with Chrome:
• Ctrl+a -> Select All
• Ctrl+x -> Cut
• Ctrl+c -> Copy
• Ctrl+v -> Paste
• Ctrl+z -> Undo
• Ctrl+p -> Print

And Chrome Adds a Bunch of New Shortcuts:
• Ctrl+? -> Chrome Help
• Alt+? -> Toggle the "?" key to/from Caps Lock
• Ctrl+d -> Bookmark this Page
• Ctrl+f -> Find Text
• Ctrl+g -> Find Text Again
• Ctrl+m -> Open the Chrome Device File System
• Ctrl+"+" -> Zoom In
• Ctrl+"-" -> Zoom Out
• Ctrl+T -> Open a New Tab
• Ctrl+TAB -> Switch to the Next Tab
• Ctrl+W -> Close the Current Tab
• Ctrl+N -> Open a New Window
• Alt+TAB -> Switch to the Next Window
• Ctrl+Shift+Q -> Sign out of Your Google Account

2.1.3 - Chrome Touchpad:

If you're using a ChromeBox, you will have to provide your own mouse. You can also use a mouse with a ChromeBook, but the ChromeBook comes with a fairly standard touchpad. There are a few touchpad gestures that you will need to know:

- To move the cursor, touch the pad and move your finger.

- To "left-click", either tap the pad with one finger or press down on the lower half of the pad.

- To "right-click", tap the pad with two fingers simultaneously or press down on the lower half of the pad with two fingers

- To scroll, touch the pad with two fingers and move them up and down to scroll vertically and from side to side to scroll horizontally

- To "drag and drop", click on the item to be dragged with one finger and then use a second finger to drag the item. Release both fingers to "drop" the item.

2.2 - The Chrome Desktop

Figure 2.2 - The Chrome OS Desktop

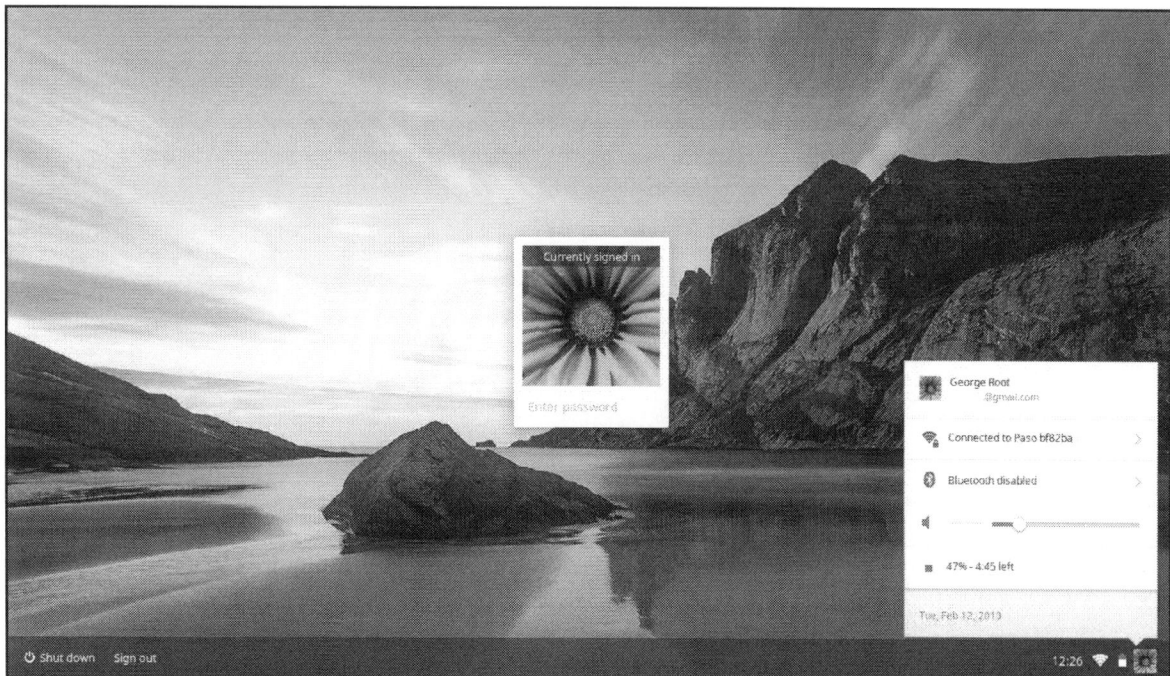

To emphasize the fact that the Chrome OS is more than just a browser, the Chrome OS running on Chrome Devices has a desktop just like your personal computer. In Figure 2.2, there is only a single user, but it is possible to have multiple users on each Chrome Device. In this case you would see a "Sign In" picture for each user. To sign-in to your Google account, just click on the appropriate picture and enter your password. When you do this, the Chrome Browser will launch and open a "New Tab".

On a Chrome Device a "New Tab" contains an array of icons showing your eight most frequently visited websites. These are intended to be quick links to your most popular sites and clicking on one will take you to that site.

With the Chrome browser running on your personal computer, a "New Tab" contains an array of icons representing all of your installed apps. There may be more than one page of these icons if you have a lot of apps. You can still reach a page of your favorite websites by clicking on the left pointing chevron at the left edge of the browser window.

You can change the Chrome desktop wallpaper image by Right-Clicking on the wallpaper area and selecting a different image. You can also import your own images.

2.3 - The Chrome Browser Window

The app that you will use most frequently on your Chrome Device is the Chrome Browser. When you launch the Chrome Browser, it will open in a new window. I have not shown the whole window here to conserve space. The "Tab Bar" at the top of the browser window is where most of the action occurs.

2.3.1 The Browser Tab Bar:

At the top of the Chrome Browser window is an area called the "Tab Bar" which looks like this:

Figure 2.3 - The Tab Bar at the Top of the Chrome Browser Window

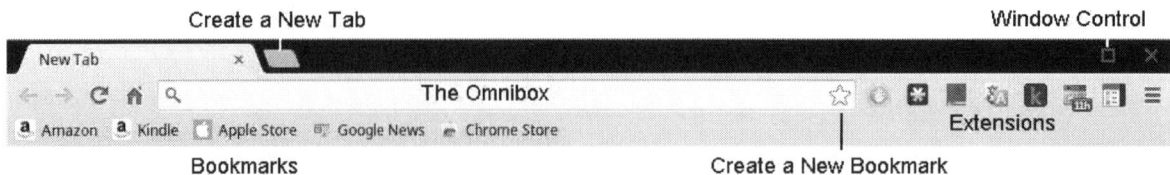

The symbol labeled "Create a New Tab" will always be just to the right of the last open tab. Clicking this will open a new tab. When you have multiple tabs open, you can arrange them by dragging them sideways.

The Omnibox is where you can enter a Google search query or a website address (URL) if you know where you want to go. You can also enter simple arithmetic expressions like (2.5*5)/13 and Chrome will calculate the answer (9.615). If you enter "about:", you will get a listing of data about your current Chrome installation.

Assuming you enter a search term, the search results will automatically include apps, bookmarks, and browsing history items that match your search query. The results will also, optionally, include related search terms and websites. You can turn this feature on and off in your "Settings". When your search results include these items, icons will appear that help you figure out which type of result it is:

- The ☆ icon appears next to bookmarked sites.
- The 🔍 icon appears next to searches, including related searches if you have the prediction service turned on.
- The ▢ icon appears next to matches from your browsing history, or related sites when you have the prediction service turned on.
- The ⬡ icon appears next to web apps you've installed from Chrome Web Store.

(this is a screenshot from a Google support page)

2.3.2 - The Browser Bookmarks Bar:

The Bookmarks Bar appears just below the Omnibox and displays the Bookmarks you have created. If you don't see the Bookmarks Bar, just open a new tab by clicking on the "Create a New Tab" icon illustrated in Figure 2.3.

Clicking on the star icon at the right end of the Omnibox will bookmark the current web page. You can also just drag the link for the page you're viewing from the OmniBox down onto the Bookmarks Bar.

You can drag and drop bookmarks in the Bookmarks Bar to arrange them as you like. If you have a lot of bookmarks, you can organize them in folders. To create a folder just right-click on the Bookmarks Bar and select "Add Folder".

To open the Bookmarks manager, right-click on the Bookmarks Bar and select "Bookmarks Manager" or type Ctrl+Shift+"O" with the browser open. You can also reach the bookmarks manager by clicking on the icon at the right end of the Tab Bar, the one that looks like three horizontal lines, and selecting "Bookmarks" from the drop down menu.

You can edit, organize, and delete bookmarks from the Bookmarks Manager or directly from the Bookmarks Bar. Right-click on the bookmark you want to change and select the action you want to take, "Edit" for example.

If you have a lot of bookmarks that you don't want to see in the Bookmarks Bar, but you don't want to delete either, the Bookmarks Manager has an "Other Bookmarks" folder. Just put these bookmarks in that folder. This folder will appear in the Bookmarks Bar if there is at least one bookmark in it.

2.3.3 - The Browser Extensions Area:

The row of small icons just to the right of the Omnibox in Figure 2.3 represent the extensions you have added to the Chrome Browser. The icon at the far right that looks like three horizontal lines leads to a drop down menu where you can select, among other things, the Settings for your account.

2.3.4 - The Google "Black" Bar

Figure 2.4 - The Mysterious Google "Black" Bar

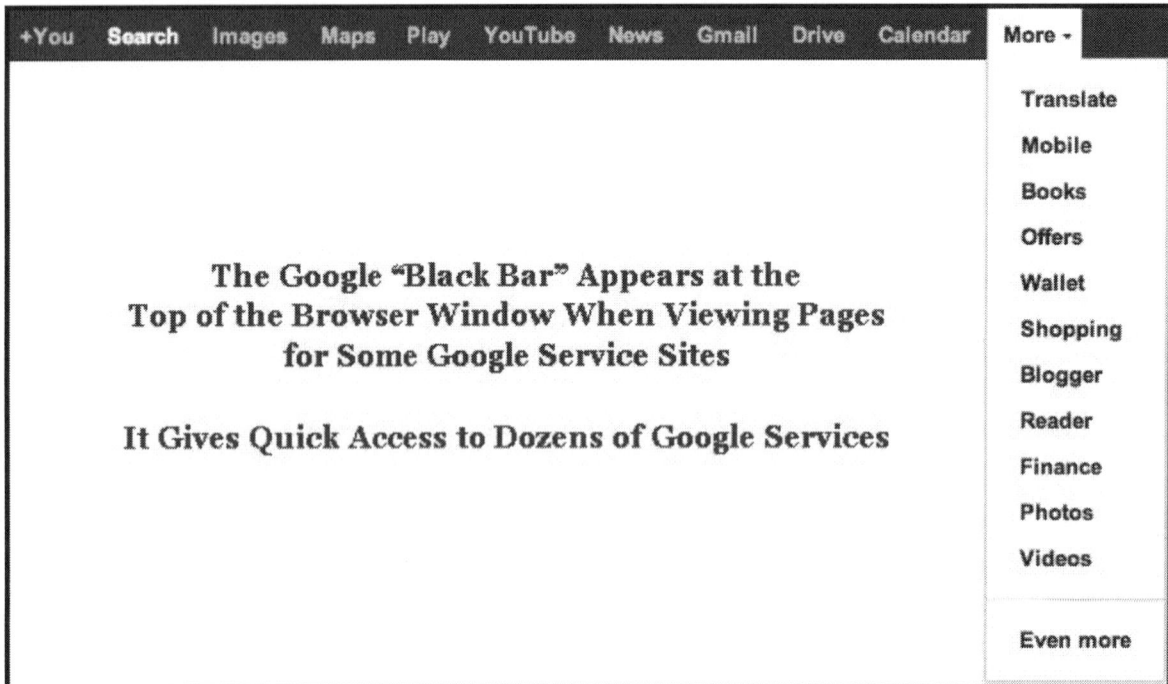

The Google Bar (sometimes called the "Black Bar") appears, when it appears, just below the Tabs Bar near the top of the Chrome Browser window. It appears when you are using some, but not all, Google services and never when you're on a non-Google site. If it is there, it gives you quick access to various Google services. Clicking on the name of one of the Google services, "YouTube" for example, will take you to that website. Clicking on the "More" button at the far right end of the Black Bar, as I have done in Figure 2.4, drops down a menu with even more services. There is even an "Even More" menu item at the bottom of this menu. Google offers a lot of services.

There is another way to access Google services very similar to the "Black Bar". It's called "Black Menu" and it is an extension that you can download from the Chrome WebStore. It gives the same instant access to Google services, but, unlike the "Black Bar" it is always there.

2.3.5 - Window Control on a Chrome Device:

Above the row of extensions in the Tab Bar at the right end of the browser window in Figure 2.3 are two small icons almost too dim to see. These are the Window Control icons. One is a small square icon and the other is an "X". Clicking on the "X" closes the current browser window.

Clicking on the square "Window Control" icon shown in Figure 2.3 will maximize the browser window and hide the Launcher Bar at the bottom of the screen. This is called "Full Screen Mode". If the browser window is maximized, clicking the "Window Control" icon will restore it to its former size. You can also maximize and restore the browser window by double-clicking in the area between the "Create New Tab" icon and the "Window Control" icon shown in Figure 2.3 or by pressing the "F4" button shown in Figure 2.1.

Dragging the little square "Window Control" icon does two things:

1) If you drag down, the current browser window will be "minimized" down to the Launcher Bar area at the bottom of the screen.

2) Dragging the "Window Control" icon to the right or left will "pin" the current window to the right or left edges of the screen.

2.3.6 - Window Control Using the Chrome Browser on Your Personal Computer

Window Control when using the Chrome Browser on your personal computer works differently than on a Chrome Device. The methods for entering and leaving Full Screen Mode are also different depending upon whether you are running the Chrome Browser on a Mac or on a Windows computer.

Chrome Browser Running on a Mac:

When the Chrome Browser window is not in "Full Screen Mode", the upper right corner of the window will have an icon that looks like two arrows pointing away from each other as illustrated in Figure 2.5. Clicking on this icon will switch to Full Screen Mode by maximizing the window and hiding the Menu Bar at the top of the screen and the Dock.

Figure 2.5 - The "Enter Full Screen Mode" Icon

To Restore the window to its previous size, hover the cursor over the top right corner of the screen. The menu bar will re-appear as illustrated in Figure 2.6. The blue icon that looks like two arrows pointing toward each other will restore the window to its previous size.

Figure 2.6 - The "Restore Window to Previous Size" Icon

You can also use the keyboard shortcut "Cmd-Shift-F" to switch in and out of Full Screen Mode.

Chrome Browser Running on a Windows Computer:

To enter or leave Full Screen Mode on a Windows computer, you have a couple of options:

1) Pressing the F11 key will enter or leave Full Screen Mode

2) Click on the Wrench icon in the upper right corner of the browser window and select "Full Screen" from the drop-down menu that appears.

2.4 -The Launcher and Status Bar

At the bottom of the Chrome Device screen, after you have signed-in, is the Launcher and Status Bar shown in Figure 2.7.

Figure 2.7 - The Launcher and Status Bar at the Bottom of the Chrome Device Screen

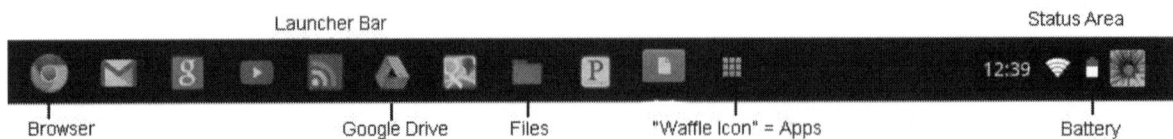

You can hide the Launcher and Status Bar by right-clicking in this area and selecting "Autohide Launcher". The Launcher and Status Bar is automatically hidden when the window is maximized. To reveal the Launcher and Status Bar again, hover the cursor over the very lower edge of the screen.

2.4.1 - The "Launcher" Bar

The left end of the Launcher and Status Bar is called the "Launcher Bar". The icons in this area represent apps that you have installed and "pinned" to the Launcher Bar. I will explain how to do this shortly. Clicking on one of these icons will launch the corresponding app. I have labeled a few of the more important of these icons in Figure 2.5. The icon at the far left launches the Chrome Browser app with a new tab.

The other three icons I have labeled don't really represent apps, but things that you will need quick access to as you work:

The Google Drive icon opens a window showing the contents of your Google Drive. Google Drive is the Chrome equivalent of the hard drive on your personal computer. It contains all of the files and documents you create. The contents of this "drive" are synced to the Google servers which is where they are actually stored. You can (should) install the Google Drive app for Windows or Mac on your personal computer. This app will allow you to access the contents of your Google Drive from your personal computer. I will discuss Google Drive more fully in section 4.

The icon that looks like a blue folder opens a window showing all of the files that belong to the current account. This includes the contents of your Google Drive as well as any files you have "downloaded" to your Chrome Device. This is basically the file manager for Chrome and I will discuss it fully in section 4. A shortcut to open the File Manager is Ctrl+m.

The last icon in the Launcher area looks like a 3x3 array of small squares (the "waffle" icon). Clicking on this icon opens a pop-up menu showing icons for all of the apps installed in your account - see Figure 2.11. You can launch any of these apps by clicking on its icon. If you have a few apps that you use a lot, you can "pin" them to the Launcher Bar by right-clicking on the app icon and selecting "Pin to Launcher". You can remove an app's icon from the Launcher Bar by right-clicking its icon and selecting "Unpin". You can also delete any app that you no longer want by right-clicking its icon and selecting "Remove from Chrome".

In the menu showing all of the apps installed in your Chrome account is one that you might find useful: it looks like a small yellow square with a light bulb inside it. This is the "Getting Started" app supplied by Google to introduce you to your Chrome Device. It's interesting. You might learn something even if you have been using Chrome for a while.

2.4.2 - The "Status Area":

At the right end of the Launcher and Status Bar (Figure 2.7) is the "Status" area showing the time, WiFi signal strength, battery charge level, and the photo associated with your account. Clicking on this photo opens a pop-up menu that you can see in Figure 2.2 and in more detail in Figure 2.8.

This is where you can Sign-Out of your session. You can change your network connection settings, enable or disable Bluetooth, and adjust the sound volume. If you click the padlock icon, that will lock the screen so that you will have to re-enter your password to resume working. The "?" icon will take you to the Chrome OS help page.

Figure 2.8 - The "Status" Pop-Up Menu

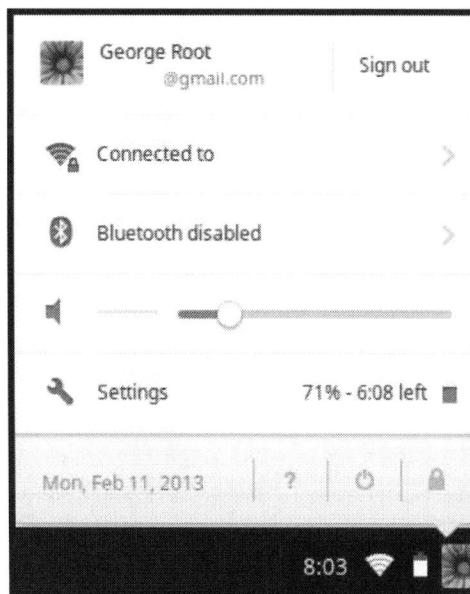

2.5 - Chrome Extensions

Chrome "Extensions" add functionality to the Chrome Browser. The icons representing installed extensions appear at the right end of the Tab Bar in the Chrome Browser as illustrated in Figure 2.9.

Figure 2.9 - Icons for Installed Extensions Appear to the Right of the Tab Bar

Figure 2.7 shows the small icons representing extensions installed on my ChromeBook. The one at the left, which looks like a stop sign with a hand in it, is the icon for the extension "AdBlock". The icons to the right of AdBlock represent, in order: LastPass, Google Dictionary, Google Calendar, Google Translate, Send to Kindle, and Black Menu.

I would like to call your attention to three of the Extensions I have installed on my ChromeBook. I'm not affiliated with any of these Extensions, I just think that they are worth their cost (they're all free):

AdBlock - (The icon that looks like a stop sign with a hand in it): This is the most popular of all the Extensions in the Chrome WebStore. It does just what its name implies - it blocks ads.

LastPass - (The black icon with a star in it): This is a very capable and secure password manager. Everything stored on the LastPass servers is encrypted, and with LastPass you keep the encryption key. Nobody has access to your passwords without this key. LastPass runs on just about every current computing device, Macs and PCs, iPhones and iPads, Android phones and tablets. You have access to your passwords everywhere you go and they are always in sync.

BlackMenu - As I mentioned above, "Black Menu", when clicked, provides quick access to many, many Google services. And, unlike the Google "Black Bar", Black Menu is always there.

2.6 - Chrome Apps

Chrome "Apps" are basically links to websites that host services that you can access from the Chrome Browser on your personal computer or your Chrome Device. These Apps appear to be running on your computer, but in reality they are running on a server somewhere in the "Cloud". What you see in your browser window are the results of these remote computations.

2.6.1 - Accessing Apps from Your Personal Computer:

If you're running the Chrome Browser on your personal computer you can access all of the apps installed there by opening a new tab by clicking on the "New Tab Icon" just to the right of the "New Tab" tab in Figure 2.10. The window that opens will contain an array of icons representing your apps as illustrated in Figure 2.10. There may be more than one page of these icons depending upon how many apps you have installed. You can scroll between these multiple pages of apps by clicking on the chevrons pointing to the right and left. You can also access the Google Apps by clicking on the "Black Menu" Extension as discussed above.

If you have a large number of apps and know the name of the one you are looking for, you can enter its name in the Omnibox and let Google find it for you.

Figure 2.10 - Opening a New Tab in the Chrome Browser Reveals Installed Apps

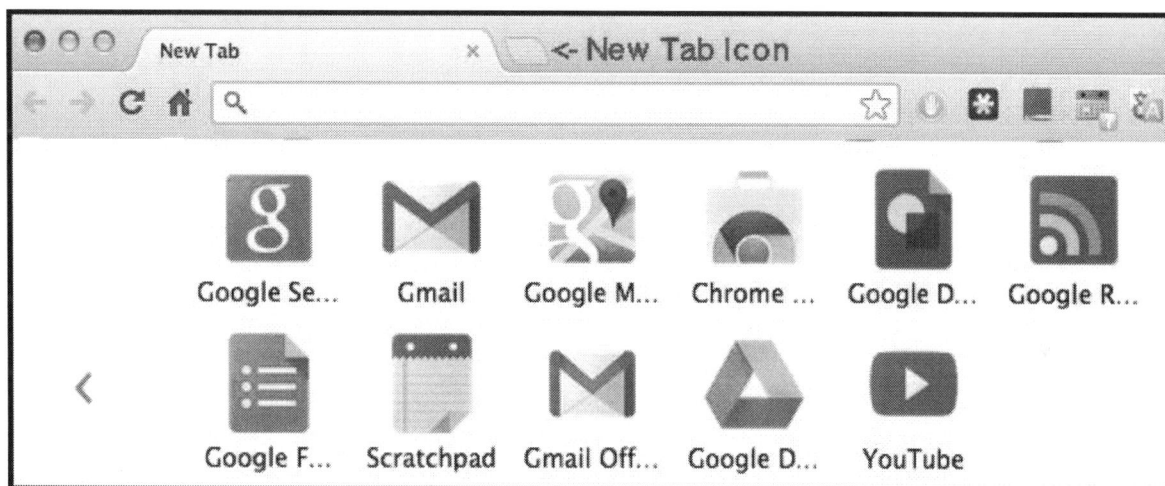

2.6.2 - Accessing Apps on Your Chrome Device:

When you open a "New Tab" in the Chrome Browser running on your Chrome Device, you won't see an array of apps. On a Chrome Device you see an array of your most popular websites. So, how do you access apps on your Chrome Device? There are two different ways to access your apps:

1) The "Launcher Bar", described in section 2.4, provides an easy way to access your favorite apps on your Chrome Device. The "Launcher Bar" is located at the bottom of the screen on your Chrome Device as illustrated in Figure 2.7. The icons in the Launcher Bar represent your favorite apps. You can launch these apps just by clicking on the icon. For an explanation of how to "Pin" and "Un-Pin" apps to/from the Launcher Bar, refer back to section 2.4.1.

2) The icon at the right of Figure 2.7, the one that looks like a 3x3 array of little squares (the "waffle" icon), opens a pop-up menu listing all of the apps installed on your Chrome Device (see Figure 2.11). You can launch an app by clicking on its icon. There is also a search box at the top of this menu. You can type a search query in this box and hit the "enter" key to find the app you are looking for, or to open the Chrome Browser and do a Google search of the web for what you entered.

Figure 2.11 - Clicking on the "Waffle Icon" Reveals All Installed Apps

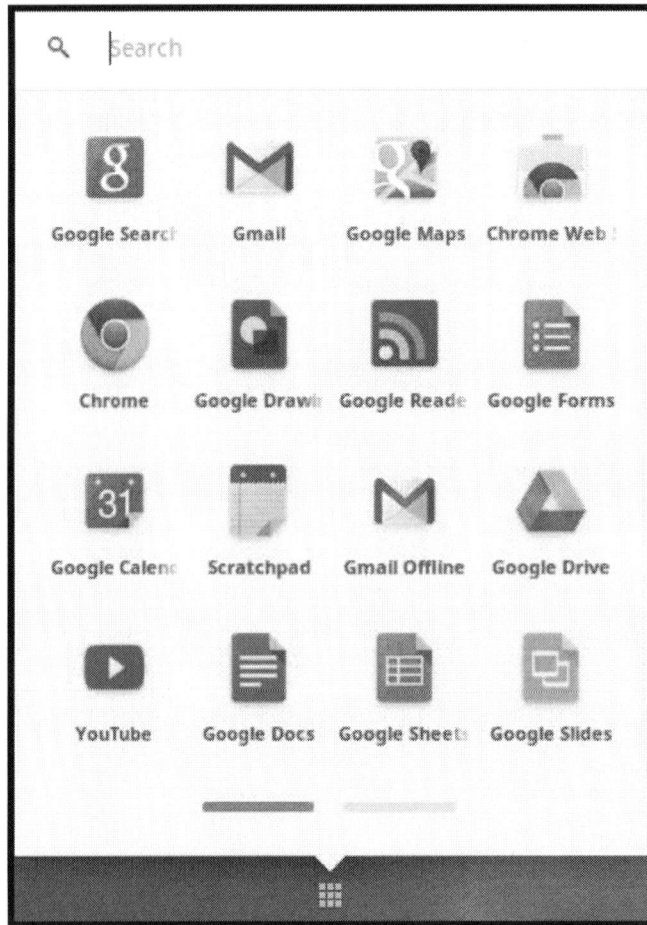

2.7 - The Chrome WebStore

You can buy apps and extensions for your Chrome Browser and Chrome Device at the Chrome WebStore which you will find here:

https://chrome.google.com/webstore/

or here:

Chrome Web Store

Remember, anyone can upload an item to the Chrome WebStore, so don't install any app or extension unless you trust its creator. Always read reviews and check the ratings before deciding if it is trustworthy.

When searching for apps on the Chrome WebStore, you can limit your research to specific categories of apps. In the upper-left corner of the WebStore page is a listing of various categories of apps. An example of this listing is shown in Figure 2.12.

Figure 2.12 - Limit Your Search to Categories of Apps

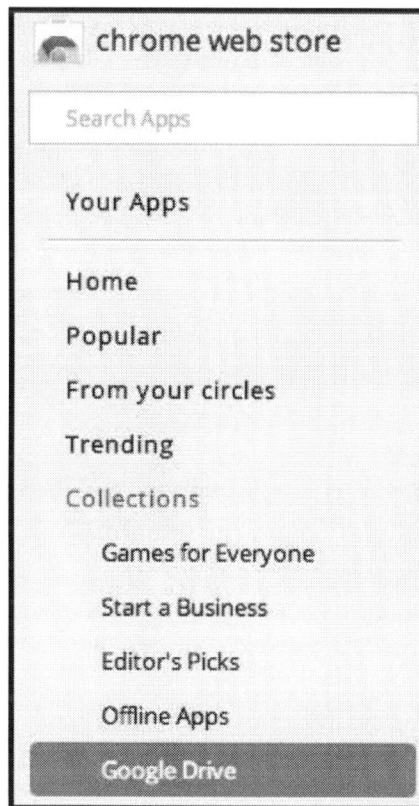

In the example illustrated in Figure 2.12, I have limited my search to "Google Drive" apps. These are apps that store their files on Google Drive and thus stay in sync even if you change computers. With the new Chrome version 25 "Create Menu" shown in Figure 7.2, these Google Drive enabled apps will appear on an equal footing with the official "Google Docs" apps. Another useful category is "Offline Apps". These apps will continue to work without an Internet connection.

If you are installing a not-free app, you will need a Google Wallet Account as well as your regular Google Account. You will be able to pay for the item with a credit card. Just click on the "Buy..." button and follow the instructions.

When you buy an item using Google Wallet, you have 30-minutes to cancel the purchase. Your credit card is not charged until this 30-minute time period expires. If you change your mind after 30 minutes, you will have to contact the developer directly for a possible refund.

2.7.1 Installing Apps:

When you find an app that you would like to install, you will see a button. If the button says:

- "Add to Chrome" -> the app is free
- "Buy for $xxx -> the app isn't free
- "Try Now" -> this is a free version of a paid app
- "Buy Upgrade" -> you have already installed the free trial version and this is the paid version
- "Rate It" -> you already have this app installed
- "Launch App" -> you already have this app installed. This is another way to launch an app.

Just click whichever button you see and the app is instantly installed, ready to run. That's all there is to it.

2.7.2 Un-Installing Apps:

If you are running the Chrome Browser you can un-install an app by opening a new tab by clicking on the "New Tab Icon" shown in Figure 2.8. Find the app you want to un-install and drag it toward the lower right corner of the page. As soon as you do this, a new button will appear it that corner labeled "Remove from Chrome". Just drop the app icon on that button and the app will be gone. You can also right-click on the app's icon and select "Remove from Chrome" at the bottom of the drop-down menu that will appear.

If you are using a Chrome Device click on the "waffle icon" in the Launcher Bar to open a pane with icons for all of your installed apps. Find the icon for the app you want to un-install and right-click on it. From the drop-down menu that appears, select the last item at the bottom "Remove from Chrome".

2.7.3 Apps:

There are thousands of mostly free apps available for Chrome.

Here are a few of those from Google:

- Gmail, Gmail Offline - email
- Google Docs - create word processing documents
- Google Sheets - create spreadsheets
- Google Slides - create slide presentations
- Google Drawings - create drawings composed of geometric figures and text
- Google Forms - create fill-in forms and questionnaires and summarize the results
- Google Drive - access your storage in the Clouds
- Google Maps - quick link to maps.google.com

• Google Reader - read your favorite rss feeds. This app will no longer be available after July 1, 2013. The popular app "Feedly" is one possible substitute.

• Google Search - quick link to google.com the search engine that made Google famous

• Google YouTube - stream millions of short videos

• Google Scratchpad - quick and simple note taking app

There are dozens more. Check them all out.

And a few more not from Google:

• Pandora Radio - create your own streaming radio station

• The Weather Channel - weather forecasts from the experts

• Kindle Cloud Reader - read Kindle books on your Chrome Device

• Numerics Calculator and Converter - a slick calculator for Chrome

2.7.4 Extensions:

There are hundreds of Extensions available for the Chrome Browser, once again mostly free.

Here are a few that you might find interesting:

• Google Mail Checker

• Google Voice

• Google Chat

• Google Tasks

• Google Translate

• Google "Email this Page"

• Google Personal Blocklist

• Google Screen Capture

And many, many more. Please note that I am not recommending any of these apps or extensions. Many I have not tried myself. These are just a few of the names that caught my interest. You can spend many happy hours browsing around the Chrome WebStore.

2.7.5 - Approve or Deny App and Extension Permissions

If a new app or extension will need access to any of your data, it must ask for your permission to access that data before it gets installed. It does this by presenting you with a dialog pane such as the one illustrated in Figure 2.13:

Figure 2.13 - The Permission Dialog

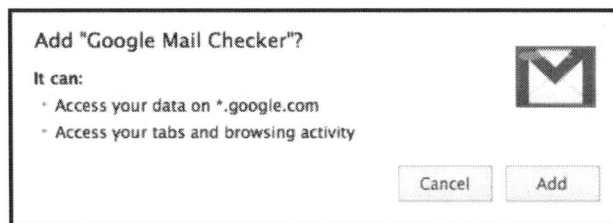

This is the "Permissions" dialog. In this case the extension "Google Mail Checker" is asking for permission to access my data on any google.com website and to access my tabs and browsing activity. I have to decide whether to grant this access by adding the app or deny the access by canceling the installation.

Here are the Permissions that the app or extension can ask for and what they mean:

Low Risk Permissions:

• **Data you copy and paste** - This item wants to read what you might put on your computer clipboard. This might include phone numbers, account passwords, or anything you might copy and paste.

• **Your location** - This might include the location of your IP address or the location of your ISP.

• **Your Tabs and Browsing Activity** - This item can see the addresses and titles of websites you visit. It can also open and close tabs and windows as well as navigate to new pages.

• **Your Browsing History** - This item can see and erase your browsing history

• **Your Bookmarks** - This item can read, change, add and organize your bookmarks.

• **Your list of installed apps, extensions, and themes** - This item can read the names of installed apps, extensions, and themes. It cannot install new items, but it can uninstall or launch items you have installed.

Medium Risk Permissions:

• **Your Data on Websites** - This item can read the web pages you visit, including your bank page, your FaceBook page, etc. Besides seeing your pages, this item can also use your sign-in credentials stored in Cookies to request or change your data from websites.

High Risk Permissions:

• **All Data on Your Computer and the Websites You Visit** - This item can do anything on your computer including reading all your files or turning on your webcam.

If all this sounds pretty scary to you, as it does to me, you might want to be very judicious in your choice of apps and extensions you install.

3 - Setting Up a New Google Account

Even if you already have a Google Account, you might want to read this Section since it discusses some topics with which you may not be familiar. Like 2-Step Verification, Application Specific Passwords, and Google Cloud Print.

3.1 - Choosing a Strong Password

The password you choose for your new Google account will become the password for your Gmail account as well as for your entire Google world. Anyone with this password will be able to access everything you have entrusted to Google from any computer in the world. That is assuming you don't set up 2-Step Verification. I will describe how to set up 2-Step Verification in section 3.3.2. But even with 2-Step Verification turned on, a strong password is still very important. One of the features Google provides when you set up 2-Step Verification is a "Trust This Computer the Next Time" button. When you click this button, Google will go through the 2-Step Verification process only the first time you use that specific computer. Thereafter, you, and anyone else, will be able to sign into your accounts on that computer using only this password. So choose wisely!

Choosing a strong password is really much simpler than you might think. The "old" recommendations were to use a random combination of upper and lower case letters along with numbers and symbols - thereby making passwords impossible to remember - thereby creating a lot of business for password manager apps.

Turns out that all of that "advice" is baloney. Mathematically, the single factor that determines a password's "strength" is the number of characters in it. "Strength" is a measure of how long it would take to break the password using any available technology. A password with 12 all lower case letters is an order of magnitude "stronger" than one with only 8 random characters using upper and lower case letters, number, and symbols.

So, choosing unbreakable passwords is really fairly simple. "ILove!Google" - 12 characters both upper and lower case and a punctuation character (!) - is an excellent password. "IReally! LoveGoogle" - 18 characters - is unbreakable yet easy to remember. Invent your own passphrase.

Hackers get passwords now, not by breaking them, but by stealing them - for example by gaining access to insecure vendor accounts and stealing the account passwords. A password manager doesn't protect against this, making their random passwords no more safe than the easily remembered variety.

The most recent password thinking is that passwords are not really that secure even if they are unbreakable, because it is getting easier and easier to just steal them via key loggers or using "social engineering" to convince the user, or a customer service representative, to give the password to the hacker.

Using a strong password is "1-Step Verification" that you are the true owner of this Google account. Google has added a second layer of security by allowing "2-Step Verification" which I will discuss a little later in the setup process (see section 3.3.2).

3.2 - Creating a New Google Account

Please note that whether you create a new Google Account or use one that you already own, the first Google Account that signs-on to a new Chrome Device becomes the "owner" of that device. The device owner has special privileges that other device users do not. For example, the "owner" can remove users from the device.

Although you can use the Chrome browser on your present personal computer without setting up a Google account, you cannot use any of the other powerful features that Chrome offers unless you create a free Google account. Even if you already have a Gmail account, you also need a Google account. Start by going to the Google account sign up page at:

https://accounts.google.com/SignUp

In the upper right corner of the page that opens, click on the big red "Sign Up" button. This will take you to the actual account creation page. The portion of this webpage where you actually enter your information looks like this:

Figure 3.1 - Start by Entering Your New Account Information Here:

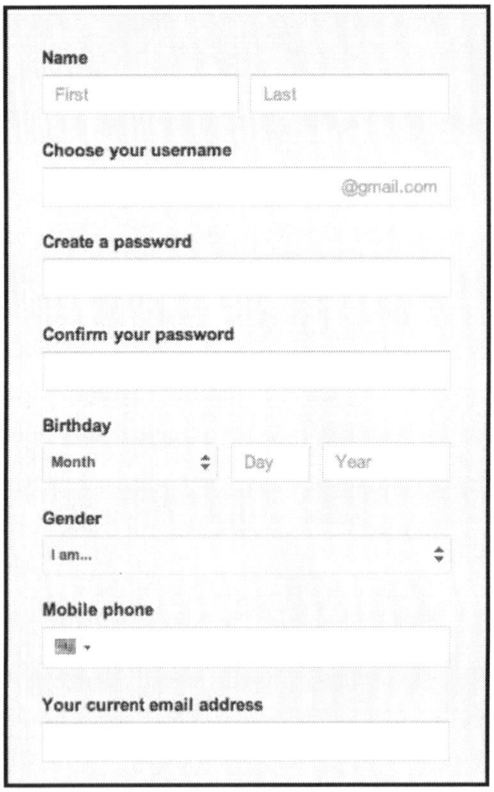

Entering your real name should be obvious, but choosing your "username" may be more difficult. You cannot have the same username as anyone else who has, or who ever had, a Gmail account. So you may have to get a little creative here. You can use letters, numbers, and "dots" in your user name. Usernames are not case sensitive so "myName" is the same as "myname".

Notice that your Gmail address is composed of the username you choose prepended to the @gmail.com domain name. You can sign-in to Google accounts using only your username. You don't have to include the @gmail.com part, although if you do everything will still work properly.

One of the most important parts of creating your Google account is choosing a strong password. I explained how to do this in Section 3.1 above. Pick a good passphrase and enter it here.

You may choose whether or not to give Google your correct birthday. I would give a false birthday close to your true one. Birthdays are becoming more popular as means to confirm your identity, particularly with health care providers, so I would not hand out this information freely. If you enter a gender, Google will refer to you as he or she. If you choose "Other" instead, Google will use gender neutral terms when referring to you. Google uses this information to send you appropriate advertising.

Giving your correct cell phone number is important because Google will use this number to send you the verification codes you will need to sign-on to your account when you have enabled 2-Step Verification. If you don't have a cell phone you can still use 2-Step Verification by printing out verification codes as I will describe shortly.

Giving your correct email address is also important because Google will send important account messages to the address you give. This cannot be the same Gmail address you are creating with this account.

Below the portion of the Account Creation page I have shown in Figure 3.1, there are a couple of more things to enter. You must agree to the Google "Terms of Service" and confirm that you are not a robot trying to create Gmail accounts from which to send spam. If you intend to use Google+ (Google's social site - like FaceBook), then you might want to enable the "Google may use my account information to personalize +1 ..." button.

After filling in all of your information, click on the big blue "Next Step" button in the lower right corner of the page. This will take you to a page where you have the opportunity to add a photo to your account. After you do this, should you choose to, click on the blue "Next Step" button which will take you to a "Welcome!" page. From here, clicking on the blue "Get Started" button will take you to your account summary page and you're good to go.

3.3 - Securing Your Google Account

3.3.1 - Turn On Encryption for Your Account

You can select which items: apps, passwords, bookmarks, etc, Google will keep in sync for you. It does this by storing your items on Google servers. You can choose whether these data should be encrypted on the Google servers.

To select which items get synced and whether or not to use encryption, follow these steps:

1) Click on the "Chrome Menu" (the 3-horizontal bar icon at the top right corner of the browser window) and select "Settings"

2) Click on "Advanced Sync Settings" near the top of the page that opens.

3) In the dialog that opens, put a check in the boxes next to the items you want to sync. Or, you can do as I did and just select "Sync Everything"

4) Select whether to encrypt just passwords, or all of your synced data. I chose "Encrypt all synced data". I don't see any reason not to.

5) In the last box choose whether to use your Google Account passphrase as the encryption key. You can also choose to use a different passphrase. If you choose to use a different passphrase, you will have to enter it every time you use a new Chrome browser. You may want to sign-in to your account from a different computer months from now, so you will have to remember this passphrase in addition to your Google Account passphrase.

3.3.2 - How Does "2-Step Verification" Work?

Two-Step Verification is relatively new to Google and some aspects of it may have changed by the time you read this. I strongly recommend that you click on the "Learn More" button in Figure 3.3 to be taken on a Google guided tour of 2-Step Verification and how it works. I will summarize the current information here, but for the latest information directly from Google, you should "Learn More".

Basically 2-Step Verification verifies that you are the true owner of the account by requiring that you have two things: 1) the correct password for the account, and 2) the cell phone whose number you gave to Google when you created your account.

So, this is how you sign in when 2-Step Verification is enabled: When you go to the Sign-In page for any Google service like Gmail, you enter your User Name (with or without the @gmail.com - it makes no difference) and Passphrase. Remember, your user name is not case sensitive, "myname" is the same as "MyName", but the password is case sensitive.

At this point you have a very important decision to make. At the bottom of every "Sign-In" page right next to the "Sign-In" button there is a checkbox labeled "Stay signed in". If you check this box, and **it is checked by default**, anyone who has access to that computer will also have access to everything you have in your Google account. No passwords, no cell phones needed. So you need to make a choice at this point, do you want your account to be secure, or do you want the convenience of never having to enter your user name and password again. If you are using a public computer such as at a library or at an Internet cafe, always, I repeat **ALWAYS**, make sure this box is not checked before you click the "Sign-In" button. If you are using a laptop, always make sure this box is not checked before you click the "Sign-In" button. If your laptop were lost or stolen anyone who has the laptop will also have access to all of your Google stuff. Personally, I always un-check this box. True I have to sign in every time I go to Google, but I am confident that nobody else can sign-in to my account.

OK. You have un-checked the "Stay Signed In" box and clicked on the "Sign-In" button. If you have entered the correct password, Google will then send an SMS text message to your cell phone. This message will be a 6-digit number. Meanwhile, back at your computer, there will be a window asking you to enter that 6-digit number. Go ahead and enter the number, but before you click on "Verify" there is another decision to make.

Figure 3.2 - You Must Decide Whether to "Trust this Computer"

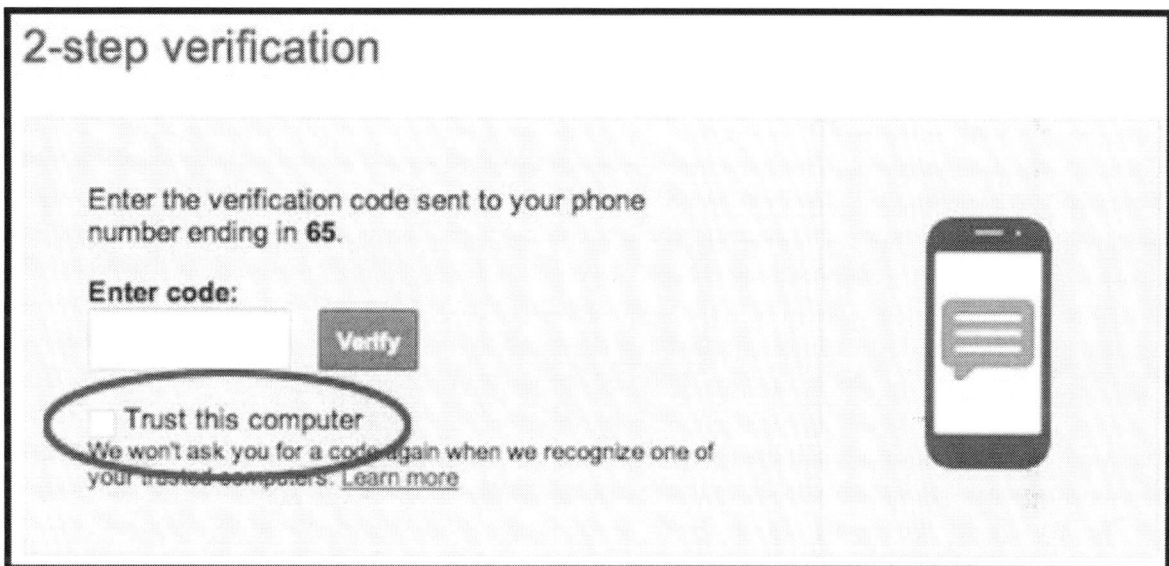

If you do NOT check the "Trust this Computer" box, you will have to go through the whole 2-Step Verification process every time you Sign-In on this computer. If you DO check this box, you will be able to Sign-In using only your user name and password in the future on this computer.

Personally, I do check the "Trust this Computer" box on my ChromeBook. It is still protected by my password and if it were stolen, I could simply change that password using a different computer and that would re-enable the 2-Step Verification process on the stolen ChromeBook. Whether or not you check "Trust this Computer", nobody else in the world can sign into your Google account from a different computer without access to your cell phone.

What if you lose your cell phone, or you don't have cell phone coverage where you need it? I'll explain how Google solves this problem shortly (see section 3.3.4).

3.3.3 - Set-Up "2-Step Verification"

OK - that's how 2-Step Verification works. Now, how do we set it up? Start setting up 2-Step Verification by going here:

<u>https://www.google.com/settings/security</u>

The account security page that opens has so much stuff on it, that I will not show the entire page, but only those portions I am going to discuss. Be sure to look at those portions that I don't discuss.

The 2-Step Verification part of the Account Security page looks like this:

Figure 3.3 - The 2-Step Verification Portion of the Account Security Page

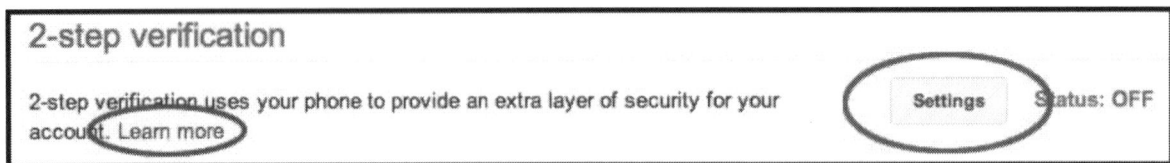

Because 2-Step Verification is relatively new, and things may have changed after I wrote this, I suggest that you click on the "Learn More" button shown in Figure 3.3 to get the latest information directly from Google.

At the right side of Figure 3.3, there is a button labeled "Settings". Click this button to take you to the 2-Step Verification Settings page. You will have to re-enter your password. And this will bring you to a dialog with a big blue "Start Setup" button. Click this button and you will finally arrive at the page where you will set up 2-Step Verification.

Setting up 2-Step Verification is a four step process:

Step 1: On the first page of this process you will be asked to confirm the cell phone number you want verification codes sent to. This will be the phone number you entered when you created your account. You also select whether you want the 6-digit access codes sent via SMS text message or by voice call. I chose the SMS message option and it works very well. I find it useful that the 6-digit code stays on the screen of my cell phone until I have time to enter it on my computer.

Once you have made your choice, click on "Send Code". This will send an access code to your phone and take you to the Step 2 page.

Step 2: On this page you will enter the 6-digit code you received on your phone. Just type it in where it says "Enter Verification Code" and click "Verify". This takes you to the Step 3 page.

Step 3: On the Step 3 page you get to choose whether to "Trust this Computer". "Trusted" computers only ask for an access code the first time you sign in. After that, they only ask for your user name and password. Google recommends "that you make this a trusted computer only if you trust the people who have access to it". Good advice! If you do "trust this computer", click on the checkbox and then click on "Next". This will take you to the Step 4 page.

Step 4: This is the confirmation page. By clicking on "Confirm", you are confirming that you really do want to turn 2-Step Verification ON for this computer and this account.

At this point you have turned on 2-Step Verification, but you're not done yet. When you click on "Confirm" on the Step 4 page, you will be taken to a page with a lot of content. I'm going to refer to this page as the "2-Step Verification is ON" page because that's what you see at the top of the page.

Once again, you will need to return to this page in the future. The easiest way to do this is to return to the account security page:

https://www.google.com/settings/security

and click on "Settings" in the 2-Step Verification portion of the page - see Figure 3.3.

This page has so much content that I will only be able to show it in pieces. Two of those pieces are critical - do not skip the next two sections!

3.3.4 - Generate and Print "Backup Codes"

You now have 2-Step Verification turned on, but suppose you lose your cell phone or you just don't have cell coverage when you need it. Google provides a backup plan called "Backup Codes". Here's the pertinent portion of the "2-Step Verification is ON" page.

Figure 3.4 - You Must Generate and Print Backup Codes

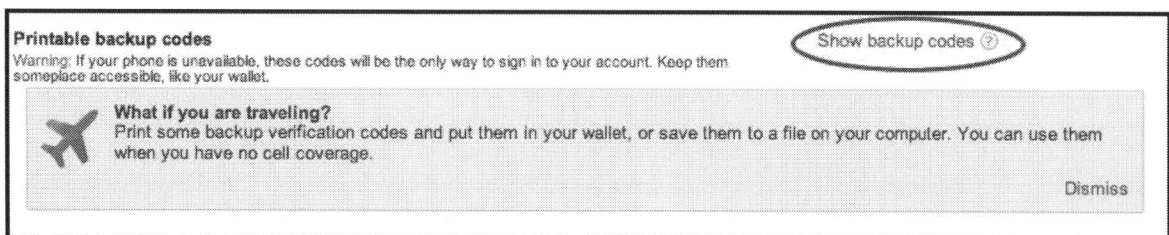

Click on "Show Backup Codes". This will generate a set of 10 Backup Codes, as illustrated in Figure 3.5, which you can print and keep in a safe place. You can use one of these codes in place of one 6-digit verification code sent to your phone. Each code can be used only once. The idea is that you will carry these printed codes with you when you are traveling and might be without cell phone coverage.

Figure 3.5 - Print One Set of 10 Backup Codes

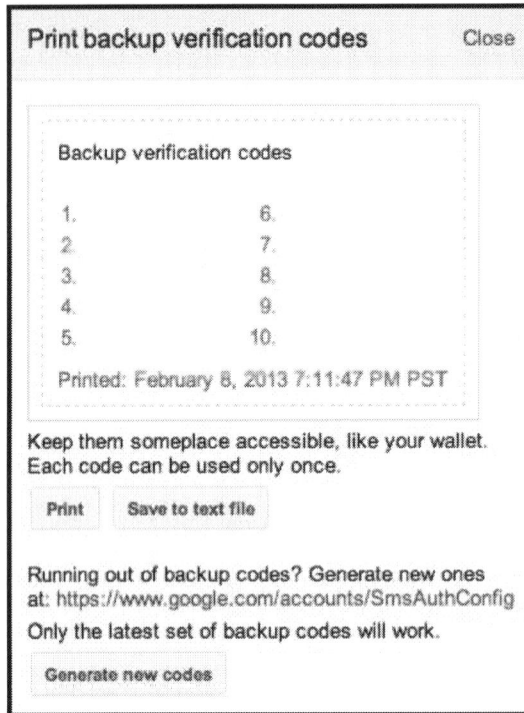

If you use all 10 backup codes or perhaps you lose them, you can generate more at:

https://accounts.google.com/SmsAuthConfig

Don't try to generate and print more than one set of 10 Backup Codes. Each time you generate a new set, the older sets are invalidated.

While we're on the topic of backup codes, Google provides another way to generate them using an app for your cell phone. "Google Authenticator" runs on Android (duh), iPhone, and Blackberry. Search for it in your smartphone app store. If you are interested in setting up Google Authenticator on your cell phone, you will find complete instructions here:

http://support.google.com/accounts/bin/answer.py?hl=en&answer=1066447

Figure 3.6 - "There's an app for that" - Generating Verification Backup Codes on Your Cell Phone

3.3.5 - How Do You Use "Backup Codes"?

It's quite simple. When you are going through the 2-Step Verification process and you come to the point where you are asked to enter the 6-digit code sent to your cell phone, but you don't have your cell phone, just enter one of the backup codes you have printed and carried with you. You have carried them with you haven't you? Each backup code can be used only once so cross off the one you used.

3.3.6 - Generate and Print "Application Specific Passwords"

Google's 2-Step Verification is a new feature of Chrome. So new in fact that some applications that sign-in to your Google account to work, including some from Google itself, are not capable of using it. Examples include: mobile Gmail, Apple Mail, Apple iOS Mail, Outlook and Thunderbird. There are also 3rd party apps that access your Google account to run properly. These include 3rd party apps that access Picasa, and Google Reader. These apps will ask for your Google password, but your actual password won't work. You have to use an "Application Specific Password" instead of your real Google password. So you must generate and print out a list of Application Specific Passwords.

To get started we, once again, return to the "2-Step Verification is ON" page. The easiest way to do this is to return to the account security page:

<u>https://www.google.com/settings/security</u>

and click on "Settings" in the 2-Step Verification portion of the page - see Figure 3.3.

Here's the pertinent portion of that page:

Figure 3.7 - Click on "Manage Application ..." to Generate Application Specific Passwords

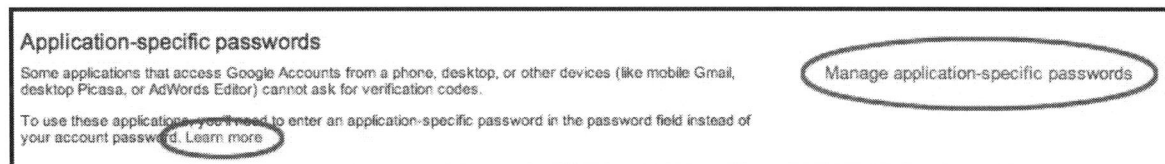

While on this page, you may wish to click on "Learn More" to learn more about Application Specific Passwords directly from Google. Click on "Manage Application Specific Passwords" to actually generate them. This will take you to Figure 3.8:

Figure 3.8 - Use this Page to Generate One Application Specific Password

Application-specific passwords

Some applications that work outside a browser aren't yet compatible with 2-step verification and cannot ask for verification codes, for example:

- Apps on smartphones such as Android, BlackBerry, iPhone, etc.
- Mail clients such as Microsoft Outlook
- Chat clients such as Google Talk, AIM, etc.

To use these applications, you first need to **generate** an **application-specific password**. Next, **enter** that in the password field of your application instead of your regular password. You can create a new application-specific password for each application that needs one. Learn more

◉ Watch the video on application-specific passwords

Step 1 of 2: Generate new application-specific password

Enter a name to help you remember what application this is for:

Name: (App 1|) (Generate password)

ex: "Bob's Android", "Gmail on my iPhone", "GoogleTalk", "Outlook - home computer", "Thunderbird"

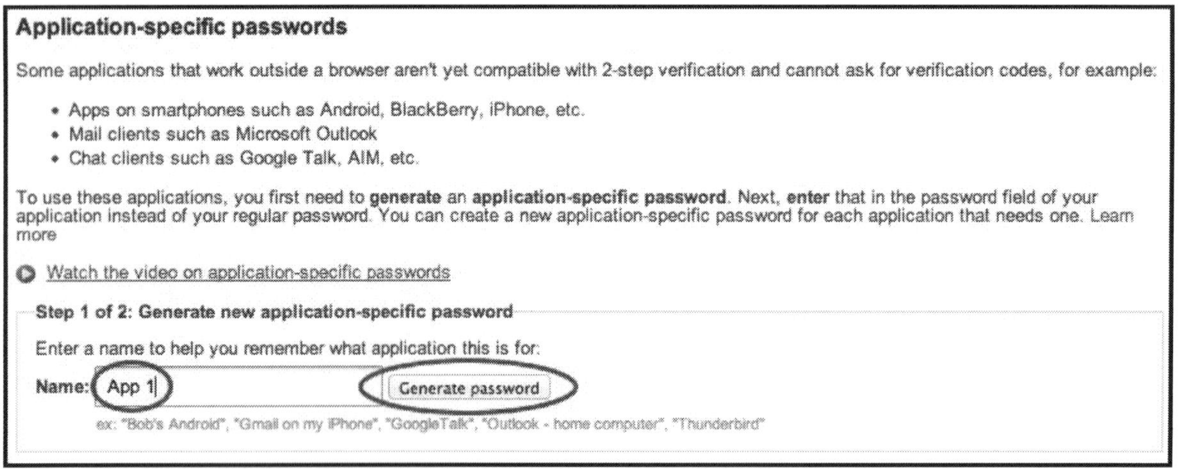

Google calls these codes "Application Specific Passwords", but the reality is that they are not specific to any particular application. So, there is no need to try and figure out how many applications you have that will require an Application Specific Password. I suggest that you generate and print at least 10 at this time. A particular Application Specific Password can be used for any application that needs one, but it can be used only once.

To generate a single Application Specific Password, type in a name - once again the name isn't important. Any Application Specific Password can be used for any application. So, to save typing, and brain cells, just type simple names. Including numbers will be useful to keep track of how many you have generated and later how many you have used.

Type a name and click "Generate Password". That will take you to a page like this:

Figure 3.9 - Application Specific Passwords Are Generated One-at-a-Time

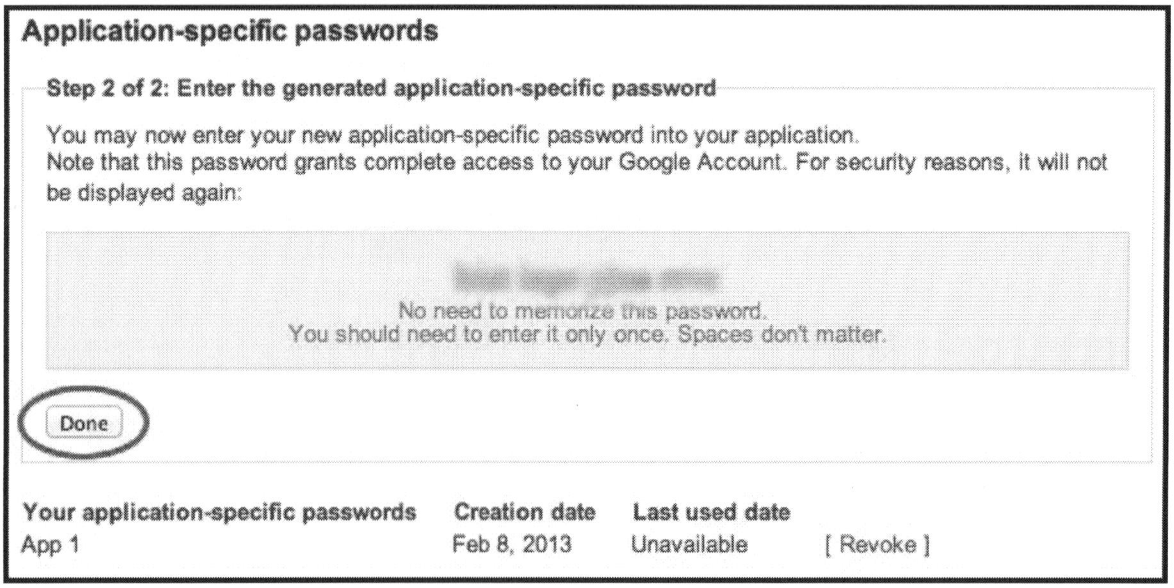

Application-specific passwords

Step 2 of 2: Enter the generated application-specific password

You may now enter your new application-specific password into your application.
Note that this password grants complete access to your Google Account. For security reasons, it will not be displayed again:

No need to memorize this password.
You should need to enter it only once. Spaces don't matter.

(Done)

Your application-specific passwords	Creation date	Last used date	
App 1	Feb 8, 2013	Unavailable	[Revoke]

When Google says "No need to memorize this password", they are assuming that you will wait until you are asked for an Application Specific Password and that you will then go through this process of generating one at that time. You would then be able to copy-and-paste the new Application Specific Password into the application asking for it. This is a pretty cumbersome process to go through, especially on your iPhone, so I prefer to generate and print several Application Specific Passwords before I actually need them.

If you choose to print a set of Application Specific Passwords, print the page illustrated in Figure 3.9 so that you will have it when you need it. When you have printed this page, click "Done" and you will be taken back to Figure 3.8 where you can enter a new name and hit "Generate Password" to create the next password. Once again, I suggest you generate at least 10 of these now.

Take care to protect these Application Specific Passwords. They are the only password needed for the app you have used them for. In addition, any of the unused passwords can be used to "unlock" any application that needs an Application Specific Password. They, in effect, bypass the 2-Step Verification process.

3.3.7 - How Do You Use "Application Specific Passwords"?

Generally you will need an Application Specific Password when you are setting up some 3rd party application that needs to access your Google Account. Applications that need to access Gmail, Google Reader, or Picasa are common. These 3rd party applications don't know anything about 2-Step Verification and cannot send a verification code to your cell phone. So, what happens?

For example, you are trying to set up your Apple "Mail" app on your iPad or iPhone to collect messages sent to your Gmail account. You have entered your correct Google Account password, but the app keeps telling you that you have used an incorrect password and it keeps asking for you to enter the correct one. After you have entered your correct Google Account password a couple of times with no success, it will suddenly occur to you, as it did to me, that this app needs an Application Specific Password. Once again, apps that need Application Specific Passwords don't know that they do - they can't ask you to enter one so you have to figure that out for yourself.

Get out your printed list of Application Specific Passwords and enter one of them. You can enter any one of them. Cross off the one you use since you cannot use that one again. If everything works as it should, your Apple Mail app will now be happy and it will be able to sign-in to your Gmail account and collect your email.

3.3.8 - Revoking "Application Specific Passwords"

If your cell phone is lost or stolen, Google recommends that you revoke your Application Specific Passwords and change the password for your Google Account. You can do this from a trusted computer. To revoke Application Specific Passwords, go to the page shown in Figure 3.8 and click on the "[Revoke]" link next to each Application Specific Password you have used. You can get to this page by following this link:

https://accounts.google.com/IssuedAuthSubTokens

3.3.9 - Returning to Your Security Settings Page

You will probably need to return to Account Security page several times. You can do this by going to:

https://www.google.com/settings/security

You can also bookmark this web page to make returning to it even easier.

3.4 - Adding and Removing User Accounts on a Chrome Device

The first user to sign-in to a new Chrome Device is the "Owner" of that device. "Owners", sometimes called Administrators on other systems, have special privileges that other users do not.

3.4.1 - Adding Users to Your Chrome Device:

You can add users to your Chrome Device from the Chrome Desktop. If you are already signed-in to your Chrome Device, sign out by clicking on the photo in the lower right corner of the screen and selecting "Sign-Out". You will then see the Chrome Desktop similar to that shown in Figure 2.2. I can't show you what the desktop actually looks like when no users are signed in because, without users, there is no account in which to save the screen shot I would have to take. You will see a desktop similar to that shown in Figure 2.2. The difference is that you will not see the "Sign Out" label near the lower left corner of the screen. Instead you will see "+ Add User". Click on this label and you can sign-in a new user to your Chrome Device. Please note that this adds a user who already has a Google Account. It doesn't create a new Google Account. You can create a new account for the new user when you are signed-in to your existing account. Then sign-out of that account and click on "+ Add User". Enter the user name and password for the new user and that user will then be able to use the Chrome Device with all of his/her own account settings.

There can be only a single user signed-in to a Chrome Device at one time. So, whichever user is currently signed-in must sign-out before a different user can sign-in.

3.4.2 - Removing Users from Your Chrome Device:

Users can be removed from a Chrome Device from the same Chrome Desktop sign-in screen as just described. Hover the cursor over the photo of the user to be removed and a small "X" will appear in the upper right corner of the photo. Click on this "X" and the user will be removed from that device. This does not delete the associated Google Account, it just removes that account from this device.

3.5 - Signing Into Multiple Google Accounts at the Same Time

3.5.1 – On Chrome Devices:

On a Chrome Device there can be only one user signed-in at a time. In order to allow another user to sign-in, the current user must sign-out.

3.5.2 - Chrome Browser Running on Your Personal Computer:

If you are using the Chrome Browser on your personal computer, it is possible to have multiple users signed-in at the same time. Here's how to do it:

1) Once you are signed-in to your Google Account, follow these steps:

2) Click on the Chrome Menu (3 horizontal bars) icon at the top-right of the Chrome Browser

3) In the drop-down menu click on "Settings"

4) In the "Users" section, click the "Add New User" button

5) Choose a picture and enter a name for this new user

6) Click "Create". A new browser window will open for this new user.

7) Sign-in to the new user's Google Account. All of the new user's synced data: apps, bookmarks, etc will be installed in this window.

You will see the picture associated with the new user's account in the upper-right corner of the browser window. Click on this picture and a drop-down menu will show pictures for all of the users signed-in to this browser. Just click on a picture and that user's window will load. Switching between users is as simple as clicking on the correct picture.

Note that this approach should only be used with other users you trust, family members for example. It is not secure because any user can access any other user's information by simply clicking on that user's picture.

If you wish to add a different user in a secure way, sign-out of the first users personal computer account and then sign-in to the new user's personal computer account. Each user will then be isolated from all other users information.

There are some Google apps that do allow multiple simultaneous Google Accounts. For example, Gmail can collect email from multiple Google Accounts. If you want to learn more about Google apps that do allow multiple sign-in, try this link:

http://support.google.com/accounts/bin/answer.py?hl=en&answer=1721977

3.6 - Signing Out of Your Google Account

3.6.1 - Signing Out on a Chrome Device:

If you are using a Chrome Device, you should see in the lower right corner of the screen a small representation of the photo you have associated with your account. Click on this icon and you will see a pop-up menu with your user name at the top. To the right of your user name is the "Sign-Out" button. Click this to Sign-Out the current user so that, for example, a different user can Sign-In.

You can also Sign-Out of the current Google Account by typing Ctrl+Shift+Q.

3.6.2 - Signing Out When Using the Chrome Browser on Your Personal Computer:

It is, of course, possible to quit the Chrome Browser just like any other app on your personal computer, but this will leave you still signed-in to your Google Account. To sign-out of your Google Account, you must be on a Google service site, such as Gmail, Google Maps, Google Drive, etc. When you are on a Google site, the email address associated with the Google Account that is signed-in appears near the top right corner of the browser window - below the Google "Black Bar" and above the "Gear Icon". Click on this email address and then click on the "Sign Out" button in the lower left corner of the pane that opens.

3.7 - Editing Your Google Account Settings

There are many "Settings" associated with your Google Account. On a Mac these would be called "System Preferences". They allow you to tune various aspects of your Chrome experience to suit your, well ..., preferences.

Accessing and editing your Settings is easy whether you are using the Chrome Browser on your personal computer or a Chrome Device.

3.7.1 - Using the Chrome Browser:

Click on the Chrome Menu (3-horizontal bars at the upper-right corner of the browser window). Near the bottom of the drop-down menu that appears, select "Settings"

3.7.2 - Using a Chrome Device:

In the lower-right corner of the screen, click on the picture that represents your account. Click on the wrench icon labeled "Settings"

In either case, this will take you to a whole world of settings that you can select to customize your Chrome Account. Here is a list of the settings and briefly, what they do:

Internet Connection
• Change WiFi networks

Appearance
• Set your sign-in screen wallpaper and get new "Themes"

Device
• Adjust Trackpad and Keyboard settings

Search
• Select your default search engine (Google of course)

Users
• Require password to wake from sleep (Recommended)

• Advanced Sync Settings:
- select what items to keep in sync

- select whether to encrypt your synced data (Recommended). I have said many times that your synced data stored on the Google servers is (optionally) encrypted. Here is where you make that happen.

- set the passphrase to use when encrypting your data. The default is to use your Google Account password.

• Manage Other Users

- enable/disable "Guest Browsing (no password required) (Disable Recommended)

- show/don't show user names and photos on sign-in screen

- Restrict sign-in to specific users. This is a good idea since it will prevent a thief from using his/her Google Account on your stolen ChromeBook (Recommended).

Date and Time
• Choose time zone
• Choose 12 hr or 24 hr clock

Privacy
• Contents Settings - manage Cookies and a lot of other things
• Clear Browsing Data - select what data to clear and then do it
• Several other privacy settings choosing what data Google may use to "enhance your browsing experience"

Bluetooth
• Turn Bluetooth on or off

Passwords and Forms
• Select whether Google should remember and fill in web forms and passwords. If you use a password manager like LastPass (Recommended) you should disable Google remembering this stuff as well.

Web Content
• Adjust font size and page zoom (Recommended for folks with poor eyesight)

Languages
• Change how Chrome handles and displays languages

Downloads
• Select where to save downloaded files
• Ask before downloading
• Enable/Disable Google Drive on this Chrome Device

HTTPS/SSL
• Manage certificates (If you don't know what this means, you don't want to do it)

Google Cloud Print
• Open Google Cloud Print (see Chapter 5)

Accessibility
• Enable/Disable: Spoken feedback, High contrast screen mode, and Screen magnifier

Factory Reset
• If you are having serious problems and you just want to start over, you can reset your Chrome Device to its original factory state.

4 - Setting Up Google Drive

4.1 - What is Google Drive?

If you are familiar with DropBox, you already know how Google Drive works. "Google Drive" is in reality a block of storage space on Google's servers. You can store any type of file in your Google Drive although it is primarily intended as the storage location for any Google documents you create using the Google apps "Docs", "Sheets", "Draw", "Forms", and "Slides" as well as any that Google will add in the future.

You can access your Google Drive from any computer with internet access. Any files you put in the Drive can be accessed from any computer with internet access. Any changes you make to the contents of your Drive are automatically synced to the Google servers and thence to any computers with access to your Drive.

There are three ways to access your Google Drive:

> 1) Using any Web Browser (section 4.2)
> 2) Using your Chrome Device (section 4.3)
> 3) Using Your Personal Computer (section 4.4)

4.2 - Accessing your Drive Using Any Web Browser

Using any web browser, go to:

https://drive.google.com/#my-drive

After signing-in to your Google Account, you will see the contents of the Google Drive associated with that account as illustrated in Figure 4-1. In this figure, my Drive contains only a single item: a folder named "Scratchpad".

Figure 4-1 - Google Drive Appears the Same on the Web and on a Chrome Device

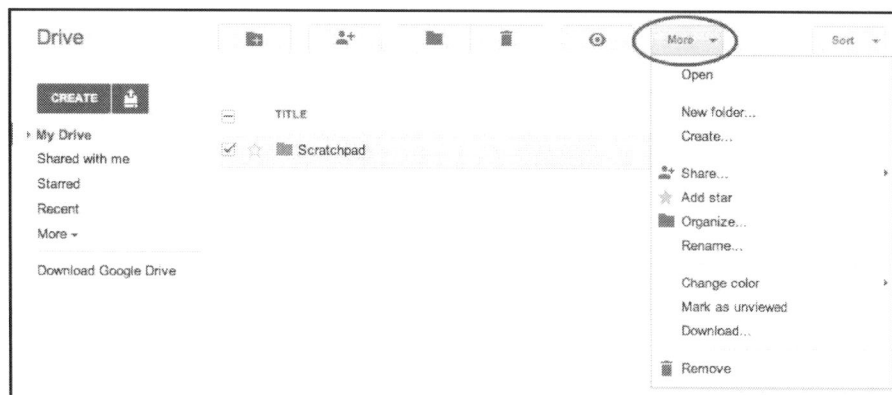

To open a file or folder simply click on it. Or click on the drop down "More" menu shown outlined in red in Figure 4.1 and select "Open". There are several other actions you can perform as illustrated in Figure 4.1.

To download a file or folder from Google Drive to your personal computer, first click on the checkbox next to the file or folder as I have done with the folder "Scratchpad" in Figure 4.1. Now click on the "More" menu button. Near the bottom of the menu list is "Download…". Clicking this will download the file to your personal computer and put it wherever you have chosen to put downloaded files - usually the "Downloads" folder on a Mac. If the file you have chosen is a "native" Chrome document: Doc, Sheet, Slides, you will have the opportunity to convert that file into Microsoft Office compatible format: Word, Excel, PowerPoint, or to a PDF file so that you can work on it on your personal computer.

4.3 -Accessing your Drive from your Chrome Device

On your Chrome Device, Google Drive is already installed and is represented by a yellow, green, and blue triangular icon that looks like the left pane in Figure 4.2. Google Drive appears to be an app in the Launcher Bar at the bottom of the screen - see Figure 2.7. When you click on this app icon, a window opens showing the contents of your Google Drive. This window looks and acts exactly the same as if you had accessed it using a web browser. In reality, that's exactly what you did - remember, Chrome is basically a web browser and Chrome "apps" are really mostly links to websites. So, the Google Drive "app" is just a link to the same website I gave you at the beginning of section 4.2.

4.4 -Accessing your Drive from your Personal Computer

You can install the Google Drive app on your personal computer even if you don't own a Chrome Device. It is included - at least the first 5 GB of storage - is included free when you sign up for a Google Account. You can download the Drive app for Mac, PC, iPhone/iPad, or Android device here:

https://www.google.com/intl/en_US/drive/start/download.html

When Google Drive first runs on your personal computer it asks you to sign-in to your Google Account. This links that Drive to that account. Any computer signed-in to that Google Account will have access to the contents of that Drive. So, you can put a file into your Drive on one computer and then take it out on another computer. That is how I have transferred the screen shots in this book from my ChromeBook to my Mac. It is almost magical.

On your personal computer, Google Drive is composed of two parts: the Google Drive app which you have to download and install just like any other app (see the link above) and a "Google Drive Folder" representing your storage space on the Google servers. The icons for this app and folder on my Mac are shown in Figure 4.2.

Figure 4.2 - The Google Drive App and Folder Icons

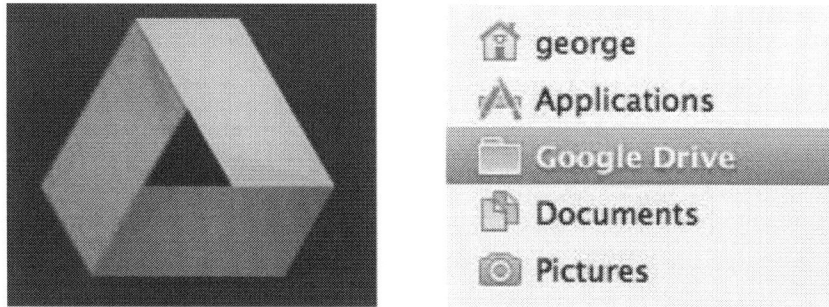

The "Google Drive Folder" isn't really a folder, it just acts like one. You can drag files into or out of this "Google Drive Folder" just as if it were a real folder in your personal computer file system. If you drag a file into the "Google Drive Folder" it is actually sent off to the Google servers somewhere in the cloud and a link to that file is stored in the folder on your personal computer . If you drag a file out of this "Google Drive Folder" it is sent back to your personal computer and removed from the Google servers. The "Google Drive Folder" is installed at the same level in your personal computer file system as your "Documents" folder on a Mac.

4.5 - Working with Google Drive on a Chrome Device

On a Chrome Device there are three types of files:

   1) Those that reside "in the cloud" on Google servers,

   2) Those that actually reside on your Chrome Device itself, and

   3) Those that are stored on an external memory card that you may have inserted into the card reader slot on your Chrome Device.

As I have said, there is very limited storage on a Chrome Device so most of your files will actually be stored on Google servers in your Google Drive.

The files that are actually stored on your Chrome Device "live" in a folder named "Downloads". The idea here is that files you create on your Chrome Device get stored automatically in your Google Drive. Any other files, such as those you download from your personal computer or from an attached memory card, get stored in your "Downloads" folder.

All of these files, locally resident as well as those on Google Drive, are managed by a Chrome app named "Files". There are two ways to open the "Files" app on your ChromeBook:

   1) Clicking on the "Files" app icon (the little blue folder) in the Launcher Bar - see Figure 2.7.
   2) Typing the keyboard shortcut Ctrl+M.

This opens the Chrome file system window as illustrated in Figure 4.3:

Figure 4.3 - The Chrome "Files" Window on a Chrome Device

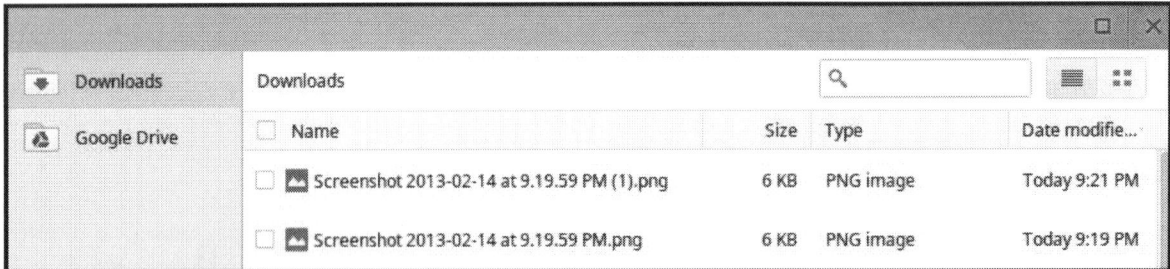

In the left sidebar in Figure 4.3 you see the two top level folders, "Downloads" and "Google Drive". If I had inserted an external memory card, that would show up here as well. Click on any of these top level folders and the resulting window will show the contents of that folder. In Figure 4.3, I have clicked on the Downloads folder revealing that there are two files in that folder - two screenshots.

When I take a screenshot on my ChromeBook, the resulting PNG (Portable Network Graphics) image file is stored in the "Downloads" folder. The files in my "Downloads" folder are stored on and are accessible only on my ChromeBook. In order to make them accessible from my Mac, I have to transfer these files to my Google Drive folder. There are two ways to do this. First, click in the checkbox next to each file I want to move. Then:

1) Simply drag any selected file and drop in onto the Google Drive folder, or

2) Right-click on any selected file in the Downloads folder and select "Copy", then open the Google Drive folder. Right-click on an empty space and select "Paste".

Copy and paste leaves the files in the Downloads folder whereas the drag-and-drop approach deletes the files from the Downloads folder. Now that the files are in my Google Drive folder, they will be sent to the Google servers from where I can retrieve them on my Mac.

In theory, if I open the Google Drive folder on my Mac I should see the two files there waiting for me. So far, this hasn't happened. What I have found is that I have to actually run the Google Drive app on my Mac in order to force a sync with the Google servers. When I double click on the icon for the Google Drive app, nothing apparent happens. But, now when I return to my Google Drive folder, the files actually are there waiting for me.

4.6 - Downloading Files to Your Personal Computer

Google Drive can export Google "Office-like" files: Docs, Sheets, and Slides, as the corresponding Office file types: Word, Excel, and PowerPoint. So, you could start one of those documents on your Chrome Device and then transfer it to your personal computer where you could continue working on it using one of your personal computer apps like "Word" or "Pages". In fact, if you transfer a "Google

Docs" document to your personal computer, you must choose what file type you want that file converted into. There are no native apps for personal computers that can open Google documents so you must convert them into a format that can be opened on your personal computer. Figure 4.4 shows your choices when you download a Google Docs (word processing) file. If you were downloading a Google Sheets (spreadsheet) file, your choices would include Excel. Similarly, if you were downloading a Google Slides file, your choices would include PowerPoint. Mac users can then open these "Office" files using Pages, Numbers, or Keynote.

Figure 4.4 - When You Download a Google Document to Your Personal Computer, You Must Choose What File Type You Want that Document Converted to

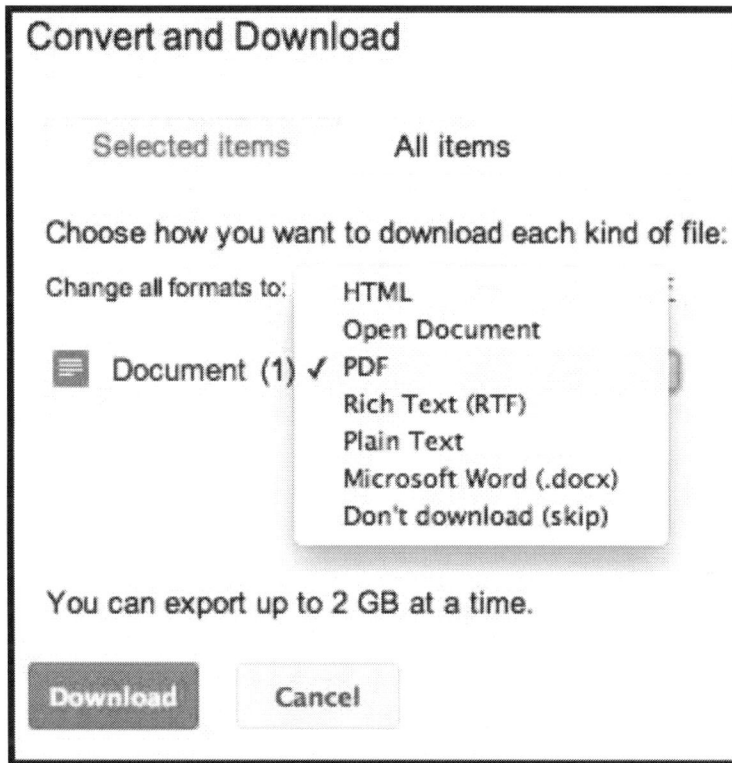

Note that if you leave the document in Google Drive, you can continue to work on it using the original Google app on the web. Only if you decide to download the file to your personal computer, thereby taking it out of Google Drive, do you have to convert it into a personal computer file type.

4.7 - Uploading Files from Your Personal Computer

In Figure 4.1, just to the right of the big red "Create" button, is a button that looks like an arrow pointing upwards out of a hard drive. Clicking on this button will upload a file from your personal computer's file system into Google Drive.

When uploading files from your personal computer to Google Drive, you have the option to convert "Office-like" files to their corresponding Google file types: Word files -> Google Docs files; Excel files -> Google Sheets files; PowerPoint files -> Google Slides files. You need to do this if you want to be able to open and work on these files using Google apps on the web.

Google has recently purchased "QuickOffice" with plans to integrate it into Google Drive. This will give Chrome users the ability to work directly with Microsoft Office files without having to convert them into Google Docs formats.

You can set-up your conversion preferences before you start uploading files. To do this, go to your Google Drive page. In the upper right corner of the Drive page, click on the "gear" icon. This will drop down a menu as illustrated in Figure 4.5:

Figure 4.5 - Upload Settings Menu

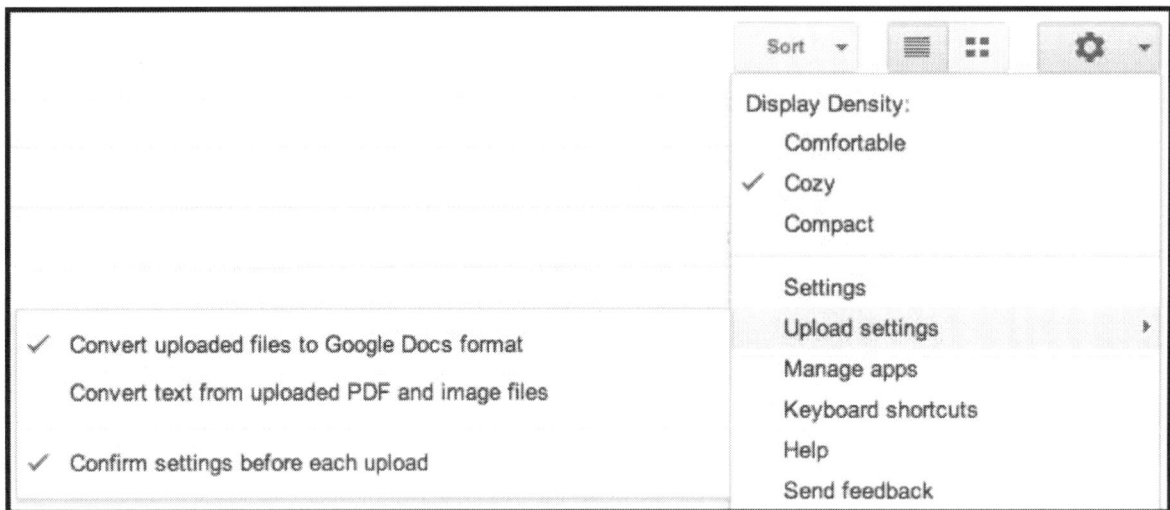

Click on "Upload Settings", as illustrated, and then make your choices in the side menu that slides out to the left. I have checked the "Convert uploaded files to Google Docs format" option. I would recommend that you check the "Confirm settings before each upload" option so that you get to choose whether to convert or not each time you upload a file.

When you click the "Upload" button, the first choice you make is whether to upload a file or a folder of files. Choosing "File" opens a pane showing your personal computer's file system from which you can choose the file to upload. If you have chosen to "Confirm Settings before each upload" as illustrated in Figure 4.5, you will be given the opportunity at this point in the upload process to convert or not to convert. If you are uploading a Word, Excel, or PowerPoint file, the conversion will take place and you will see the corresponding Google document in your Google Drive. Clicking on one of these uploaded files will launch the appropriate Google app.

At this time, Google cannot convert the Mac Pages, Numbers, or KeyNote file types. If you do upload one of these files, it will be uploaded in its Mac file format (i.e. you will not be able to open it with Google apps). The work-around, at least until Google adds the functionality to convert Pages,

Numbers, and Keynote files, is first to export those files on your Mac to the corresponding Office-like file types. So, for example, if you have a Numbers document that you would like to upload so that you can use Google Sheets to collaborate on its editing, you would first open the file in Numbers and then export it as an Excel file. You will be able to upload this file type to Google Drive and continue working on it with Google Sheets.

4.8 - "Preview" in Google Drive

With Chrome version 25, Google has introduced a "Preview" feature to files you have in your Chrome file system. "Preview" will open automatically when you click on image files, videos, and PDF files. These Previews will show you what the contents of that image, video, or PDF file look like without having to open an app that handles that type of file. If you want to Preview a "Google Docs" file without actually opening it, just right-click on the file name and select Preview.

The main purpose of Preview is to allow users to find the file they are looking for based on the contents of the file. You can select the proper image, for example, by seeing what the images actually look like. Once the Preview window is open, you can move from file to file by clicking on the right and left facing arrows at the sides of the window. If you have a multipage PDF file, you can scroll through the pages in Preview. You can watch a video file right in the Preview window. You can also perform several actions on the Previewed file such as: print it, copy text, download the file, or open the file in an app that can edit it.

Mac users may recognize all of these features from the homonymous (I'll save you the trouble - it means "with the same name") app on Macs.

4.9 - What Else Can You Do with Google Drive?

OCR - When you upload a PDF or image (.jpg, .gif, or .png) file that contains an image of text, Google Drive can perform Optical Character Recognition (OCR) on that text and yield a fully editable text document. The image of text might have been created by scanning or photographing a page of text, for example. For successful OCR your text image must meet some requirements. High resolution images are required - characters at least 10 pixels high. The text must be right-to-left and horizontal. Rotate images if necessary before uploading them. Text must, at this time, be composed of Roman characters. Common fonts such as Arial and Times New Roman work best. Maximum file size is 2 MB and only the first 10 pages of a PDF document will be OCRed. Character recognition might take a minute or longer so be patient.

Host Webpages - You can host a website on Google Drive by:
1) Create your website using HTML, CSS, and Javascript.
2) Create a new folder in your Google Drive and share it as "Public on the web".
3) Upload your HTML, CSS, and Javascript files to this folder.
4) Open the HTML file and click the "Preview" button in the ToolBar.
5) Copy the URL that looks like: "www.GoogleDrive.com/host/ ..." and send it to anyone you want to see your webpage.

5 - Setting Up Google Cloud Print

At this time, Google Cloud Print (beta) is a work in progress. New features and apps that can print from your Chrome Device are being added regularly. I expect that some things will have changed by the time you read this. To check up on the latest status of Google Cloud Print go to:

https://google.com/cloudprint

One of the things that makes it possible to build a Chrome Device with only 16 GB of memory is that it doesn't contain print drivers for the thousands of printers currently in use. In fact, the Chrome OS has only a single print driver - one for "Google Cloud Print". Of course, if you are running the Chrome Browser on your personal computer then you can use the print facilities of your personal computer. With a Chrome Device, you print to Google Cloud Print instead.

Since your print jobs travel from your computer up to the Google servers and back down to your printer, you may be concerned about security. All of these communications, both to and from the Google servers are encrypted (https://). The document being printed is kept on the Google servers only as long as it takes to complete the printing. When printing is done, your document is deleted from the Google servers. However, a record of the print job: name of document, your Google ID, printer used, and printer status are retained by Google.

There are three types of printers you can print to from Google Cloud Print:

5.1 - Printing to Cloud Print Enabled Printers

At the time this is being written, Cloud Print enabled printers are made by Canon, Dell, Epson, HP, and Kodak. If your Chrome Device is your only personal computer then you might want to invest in a Cloud Print enabled printer from one of these vendors. Your Cloud Print printer must be connected directly to the internet, no personal computer is required. The printer is assigned an unique email address. When you want to print something from your Chrome Device, you email the document to your printer's email address. For instructions on how to set up and use one of these Cloud Print Enabled printers, refer to the instructions that came with the printer.

5.2 - Printing to Printers Connected to Your Personal Computer

You can "share" the printers already attached to your personal computer - Mac or Windows - so that you can print to them from your Chrome Device. To do this your computer must be connected to the internet and you must have the Chrome Browser installed on your personal computer and that browser must be attached to the same Google Account as the Chrome Device you are printing from.

So, the **first step** in setting up a shared printer for your Chrome Device is to download and install the Chrome Browser on your Mac or Windows computer if you have not already done that. You can download the Chrome web browser free from the Google site

https://www.google.com/intl/en/chrome/browser/

The **second step** in setting up a shared printer for your Chrome Device is to enable sharing of the printer(s) attached to your personal computer. For example, on a Mac:

1) Go to "System Preferences" and open the "Sharing" preference pane.

2) Click on "Printer Sharing" and then click on the checkboxes next to the printers you want to share.

On a Windows 7 PC it's a little more complicated:

1) Click "Start"

2) Click "Control Panel"

3) In the Search Box, type "Network"

4) Click "Network and Sharing Center"

5) In the left pane, click "Change Advanced Sharing Settings"

6) Click the down pointing chevron to expand the network profile

7) Turn on File and Printer Sharing if it isn't already on

8) Click "Save"

9) Now, Click "Start" again

10) Click "Devices and Printers"

11) Right-click the printer you want to share and select "Printer Properties"

12) Click the "Sharing" tab

13) Check the "Share this Printer" checkbox

The **third step** is to add the shared printers to the "Google Cloud Print Connector" that is built into the Chrome Browser on your personal computer - Mac or Windows.

1) Sign-in to the user account on your personal computer that contains the Chrome Browser that is signed into the Google Account that you want to print from on your Chrome Device.

2) Launch the Chrome Browser

3) Click the "3-horizontal bar" icon near the upper right of the window and select "Settings"

4) Click "Show Advanced Settings" near the bottom of the Settings window

5) Scroll down to "Google Cloud Print"

6) Click "Add Printers". If no printers are connected to this Google Account this link is titled "Add Printers". If a printer is connected, this link is titled "Open Google Cloud Print".

7) If prompted, Sign-In to the same Google Account that you will be printing from on your Chrome Device. If you have set up 2-Step Verification you will use one of your Application Specific Passwords instead of your regular account password at this point.

8) Click on the blue button "Add Printers". This adds all the printers shared by this personal computer to this Google Account.

6 - Print Using Google Cloud Print

First, if you are printing to a printer attached to your personal computer and shared via "Google Cloud Print Connector" with your Google Account, make sure that both the personal computer and the printer are turned on. Also make sure you are signed-in to the same Google Account as the Google Cloud Print Connector.

6.1 - Apps that Can Print to Google Cloud Print

At this time not all apps support printing to Google Cloud Print. There are several apps that can print to Google Cloud Print and there will undoubtedly be more by the time you read this. Here are a few of those currently available (this is not an exhaustive list):

6.1.1 - On any Device:

Chrome Browser - You can print any open tab in the Chrome Browser by hitting Ctrl+P or Cmd+P on a Mac to open the Print Dialog. You can also reach the same Print Dialog by going to the Chrome Menu (3-Bar Horizontal Icon at the upper-right corner of the Chrome window) and selecting "Print". This will allow you to choose a destination printer, select the range of pages to print, the number of copies, Portrait or Landscape orientation, and whether to include headers and footers.

6.1.2 - On Your Android Device:

Cloud Print Beta - Print files from your Android device, including emails and attachments, text messages, contacts, web pages, documents, etc.

Cloud Printer - If you use Firefox on your mobile phone, Cloud Printer allows you to print web pages.

6.1.3 - On Your iOS Device:

PrintCentral Pro - Allows you to print emails and attachments, contacts, web pages, text messages, and more.

6.1.4 - On any Mobile Device:

Mobile Google Apps - If you access Gmail or Google Docs through your phone's browser, you can print any email, document, spreadsheet, or other Docs file through Google Cloud Print.

6.1.5 - On Your Mac or Windows PC:

Cloud Printer - Cloud Printer allows you to print from any application on your Mac through the regular Mac print menu.

Cloud Print for Windows - Print documents from your Windows PC to any of your cloud printers.

6.2 - Printing the Current Web Page

Printing the current web page - what you are looking at on the screen - is easy:

Type Ctrl+P or go to the Chrome Menu (3-Bar Horizontal Icon at the upper-right corner of the Chrome browser window) and select "Print...". This will bring up a "Print Dialog" showing a list of the available print destinations - see Figure 6.1. These include shared printers ("BW" in the figure), your local FedEx office, and "Save to Google Drive".

Figure 6.1 - Choose the Print Destination in the Print Dialog

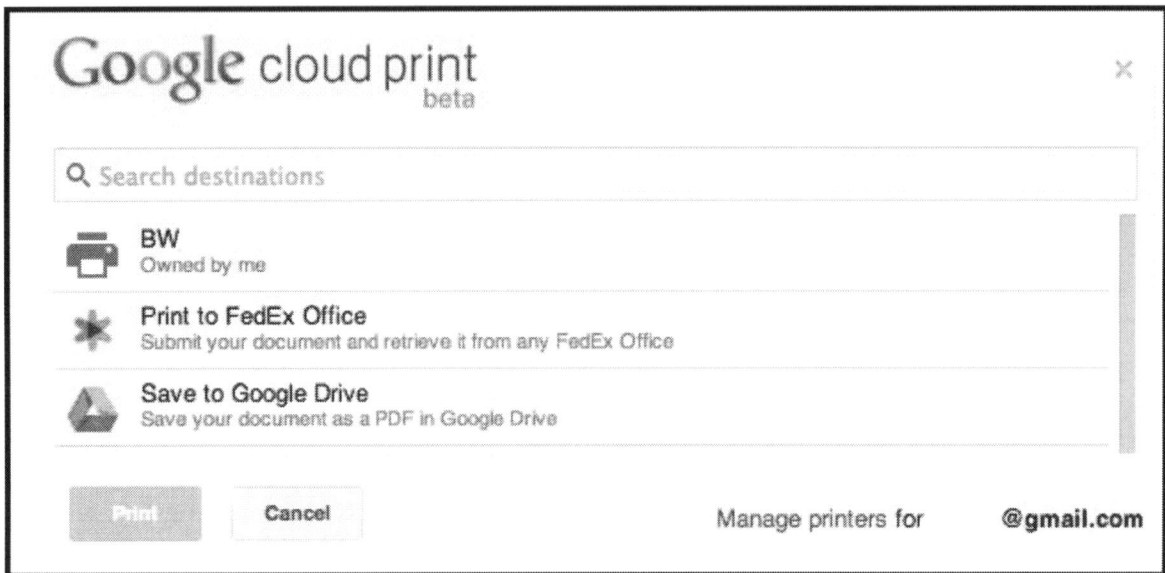

Select the destination you want and click the "Print" button that appears.

If you have selected a printer attached to your personal computer, it should start up and print the page. It may take a few moments because the print job has to travel over the internet to the Google servers and then back to your personal computer where it is printed.

If you want to print a Google Docs document stored in your Google Drive. You can simply go to your personal computer and open the document from the Chrome Browser and print it using the personal computer print process.

6.3 - Printing a Google Doc

One of the primary uses of Chrome is to create "Google Docs": "Docs", Sheets, Slides, Forms, and Drawings. Printing any of these documents is easy. In fact the process is the same as described in section 6.2 "Printing the Current Web Page". With the Google document open:

1) Type Ctrl+p or select "Print…" from the Chrome Menu.
2) Select the destination printer if necessary
3) Click "Print"

Can't get much easier than that.

6.4 - Printing to Your Local FedEx Office

"Print to FedEx Office" is listed as one of the "printers" you can print to in the list of printers available to you (see Figure 6.1). You'll be asked to share your email address with FedEx Office and agree to the FedEx Office terms of use. If any issues occur with your print job, FedEx Office will notify you via email. Check the box "I agree" and click on the Print button. A notification box appears with a FedEx Office code that is available for use immediately and valid for up to 10 days. Use this code to pick up your document from any FedEx Office location. This is a viable option only if you have a FedEx Office nearby.

Even if you have a printer, you might find "Print to FedEx Office" useful. FedEx has printer capabilities that your printer may not have. For example, printing in color or printing on 11x17 inch paper.

6.5 - Printing to a PDF File in Your Google Drive

When you print a document, a "Print Dialog" will open with a list of available printers (see Figure 6.1). "Save to Google Drive" will be one of these printers. If you choose "Save to Google Drive" as your print destination, the page will be converted to a PDF file and that file will be put in your Google Drive. You can then sign into the personal computer user account attached to the same Google Account from which you sent the print job and you should find the PDF file in the Google Drive in that account. I have found that Google Drive doesn't always sync right away. To force a sync, find the Google Drive app on your personal computer and launch it. Nothing apparent happens, but now you will find your PDF file in the Google Drive folder on your personal computer. You can now drag the PDF file out of Google Drive and save it anywhere you choose on your personal computer. This file can be opened and printed by whatever app handles PDF files on your personal computer: "Preview" on the Mac and "Adobe Acrobat Reader" on Windows machines. This option is particularly useful if you have a printer attached to your personal computer but it isn't "connected" to your Google Account.

6.6 - Printing from the Chrome Browser on Your Personal Computer

If you are using the Chrome Browser on your personal computer, you may not need to use Google Cloud Print. If your personal computer is connected directly to a printer, then printing things from within the Chrome Browser is no different from printing any other documents on your computer.

To print something from within the Chrome Browser, you will initiate printing the same way you do it for any document - generally you go to the file menu and select "Print" or type the keyboard shortcut Ctrl+P. This will open a Chrome Print dialog as illustrated in Figure 6.2. At the bottom of this dialog you have the choice of which print dialog to use: Your normal System Print Dialog, or, if your printer is an ePrint Enabled printer, the Google Cloud Print Dialog. If you have a printer connected to your computer, just click on "Print".

Figure 6.2 - The Chrome Browser Print Window

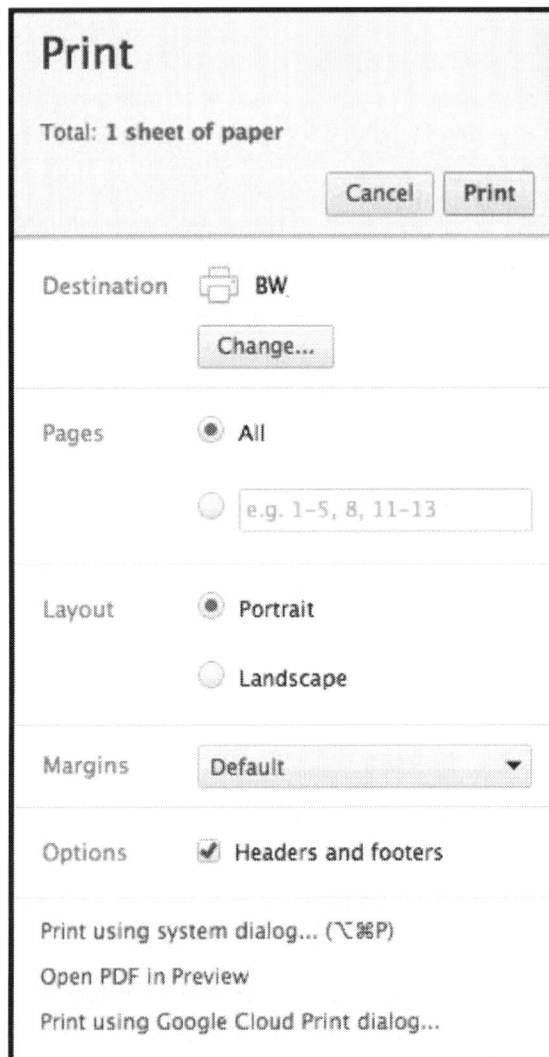

7 - Using Google Document Apps

At the time this is being written, there are five Google apps for creating documents:

• Google "Docs" creates word processing documents like Word or Pages

• Google "Sheets" creates spreadsheets like Excel or Numbers

• Google "Slides" creates slide presentations like PowerPoint or Keynote

• Google "Drawing" creates drawings composed of geometric figures, and text

• Google "Forms" creates "fill-out" forms that can be sent to people for them to fill out.

Document files created by any of these apps are automatically stored in your Google Drive. If you are working on such a document, it is automatically saved to Google Drive every few seconds. If you have granted access to your Google Drive to another person, that person can watch you create or collaborate with you on editing the document. All your files in Google Drive are backed up by Google. Automatic saving, and automatic backup. How sweet is that?

There are maximum size limits on document files created by Google apps:

• Google Docs: 1,024,000 characters. Uploaded Doc file size limit = 2 MB.

• Google Sheets: 400,000 cells and 256 columns. Uploaded Sheets file size limit = 20 MB.

• Google Slides: 50 MB (approximately 200 slides)

7.1 - Setting Up Offline Access

What if you don't have internet access? If you are using the Chrome Browser or a Chrome Device, several of the Office-like "Google Docs" apps allow offline access. This offline access does not require that you download the file to your personal computer. Google takes care of everything for you. Offline access is already set-up if you are using a Chrome Device but if you are running the Chrome Browser on a personal computer you need to set-up offline access before you can use it.

To set-up offline access on your personal computer you must have already installed the Google Drive app (see section 4.4) and you must be using the Chrome web browser, so you need to install both of those apps on your personal computer if you haven't already done that.

Now, open the Chrome Browser and go to your Google Drive on the web:

https://drive.google.com/#my-drive

At the left side of the Google Drive window that opens you will find a big red "Create" button (see Figure 7.1). Below the "Create" button click on "More". After clicking "More" you will find a menu item "Offline Docs" as shown in Figure 7.1:

Figure 7.1 - Enable Offline Viewing and Editing from the Google Drive Window

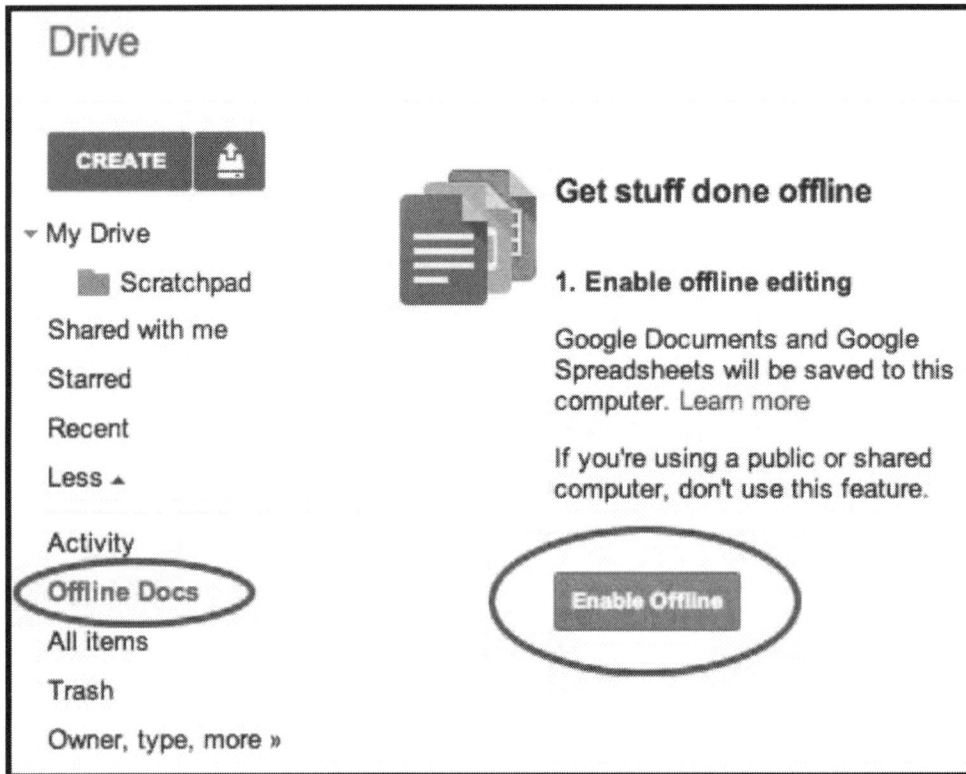

In Figure 7.1, you can't see "More" because the "More" has been converted to "Less" since I have already clicked on "More" to reveal the drop down menu containing "Offline Docs". Click on "Offline Docs" and the "Get Stuff Done Offline" panel will open as shown. Click on the blue "Enable Offline" button. Things will happen and in a moment or two you will have offline access to your files in Google Drive. Files that you can access offline will be given an "Offline" tag in the Drive window. You can view these documents without an internet connection. You can edit some of these documents offline. Right now, Google "Docs" and "Slides" can be edited while offline. Google will be expanding the number of apps that you can use offline in the future.

Remember, you don't have to set-up offline access if you are using a Chrome Device since it is already set-up on these devices.

At this time, there is an app in the Chrome Webstore, "Gmail Offline", that will allow offline access to your Gmail messages. You can read and reply to your messages, but nothing will be transmitted until web access is re-established. You can download "Gmail Offline" from the Chrome WebStore free.

There are a number of non-Google apps available on the Chrome Webstore that offer some functionality while offline. Visit the Webstore and search for "offline" or just click on the "Offline Apps" item shown in Figure 2.12. A few examples of apps that can function offline are:

- "Scratchpad" - a simple note taking app

- "Numerics Calculator and Converter" - a great app

- "Offline Dictionary"

There will be many more offline apps in the future now that Google has enabled "Packaged Apps" that can function without an internet connection.

After you have been working offline, you will have to re-establish online access once you have a connection to the internet again. A note will appear near the top of the Google Drive window that you will click on to go back to online access. This will initiate a sync and all of the changes you have made while offline will be transferred to your online Drive.

7.2 - Creating Folders and Moving Files

Before creating new documents, it might be a good idea to create folders to organize these documents. To create a new folder within your Drive, click on "Create" then on the "Folder" icon shown near the top of Figure 7.2. When you do that, the panel shown in Figure 7.3 will open allowing you to give the new folder a name. But before we go to Figure 7.3, let's take a closer look at the Create Menu in Figure 7.2. This menu has been updated in Chrome version 25.

Figure 7.2 - Clicking on "Create" Allows You to Create Folders and Documents

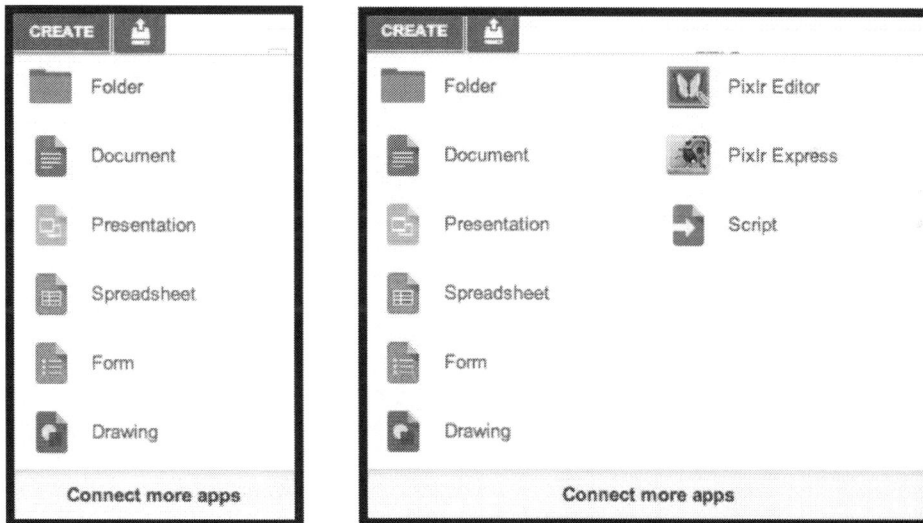

Figure 7.2 shows two versions of the Create Menu. The one on the left is the "old", Chrome version 24, menu while the one on the right is the newly introduced Chrome version 25 Create menu. The "old" Create menu lists only those Google apps that can create files (documents) in Google Drive. But there are now several 3rd party apps that also create and store their data files in Google Drive. These apps also stay in sync between devices. Recognizing this, Google introduced the new version 25 menu which allows these 3rd party apps to be listed in the Create menu to the right of the Google

apps. Apps that you install that use Google Drive as their file repository appear automatically in this new menu. You can shop for Google Drive enabled apps in the Chrome WebStore by clicking on the "Connect more apps" button at the bottom of the Create Menu.

Figure 7.3 - Give the New Folder a Name

Returning to Figure 7.3 I have named the new folder "myDocs". I will use this folder to contain the Google "Docs" I create. Repeating this process two more times and I have created three folders in my Google Drive to contain my Google "Docs", "Drawings", and "Sheets". Figure 7.4 shows these folders nested inside My Drive.

Figure 7.4 - Creating Different Folders to Hold Different Types of Documents

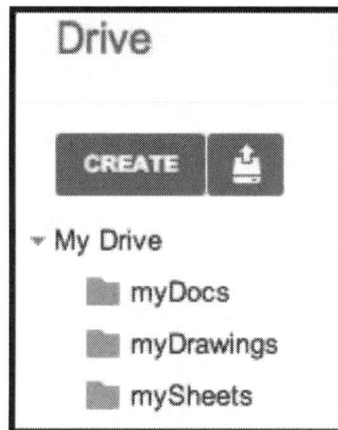

There are two other ways to create a new folder. These are illustrated in Figure 7.5.

The second way to create a new folder is to click on the folder inside of which you want to "nest" the new folder. In Figure 7.5 I have clicked on the myDocs folder to select it - it is colored red to show that it is selected. The new folder I create will be inside this folder. At this point you can simply click on the icon, outlined in red, at the top of Figure 7.5 that looks like a folder with a "+" in it. This will create a new folder inside whatever folder you selected in the left sidebar - "myDocs" in this example.

Figure 7.5 - Two Other Ways to Create a New Folder

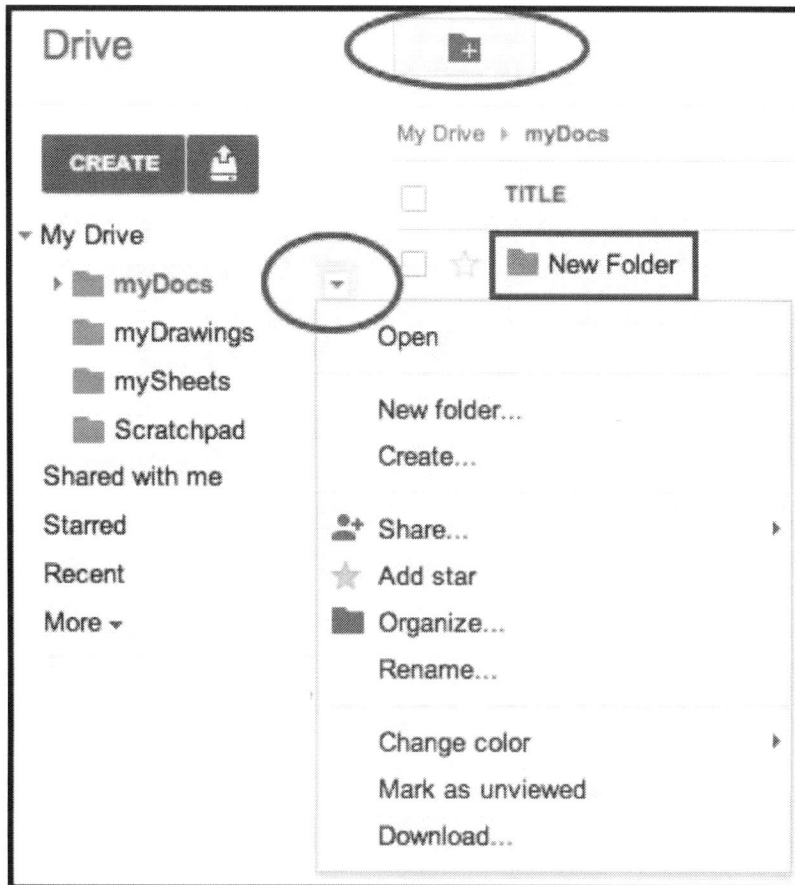

A third, slightly more cumbersome way to accomplish the same thing, is to click on the small downward pointing disclosure triangle displayed to the right of the name of whichever folder you have selected in the left sidebar. That will drop down a menu, also shown in Figure 7.5, from which you can select various actions, one of which is to create a "New Folder...". The result of either of these two approaches is the creation of the new folder outlined in blue. You could have given this folder a name during the creation process, or you could rename it now by selecting "Rename..." from the drop down menu.

7.3 - Sharing Google Documents

One of the really great advantages of Google's cloud computing approach is that it is easy to share documents and collaborate with other people while creating or editing any of the "Google Docs" documents. If two people are sharing a document, each can see, in (near) real time, any changes the other person makes. More Google magic!

Sharing and collaborating on documents is easy. Open your Google Drive (read the first few paragraphs of section 7.4 if you don't know how to do this). There are two ways to start the sharing process.

One way is to select the document (file) you want to share by clicking the checkbox to the left of the name of the file in Google Drive. This will enable a new set of icons along the top of the Drive window as illustrated in Figure 7.6:

Figure 7.6 - The Icon Strip That Appears When You Select a File in Google Drive

The second icon in Figure 7.6, the one that looks like a head and shoulders with a "+" sign next to it , is the one you want. Click on this icon to start the sharing process. Or, even easier, just right-click on the file you want to share and select "Share" from the drop-down menu that appears. Performing either of these actions opens a "Sharing Settings" window as illustrated in Figure 7.7.

Figure 7.7 - The Sharing Settings Window Let's You Select Whom to Share With

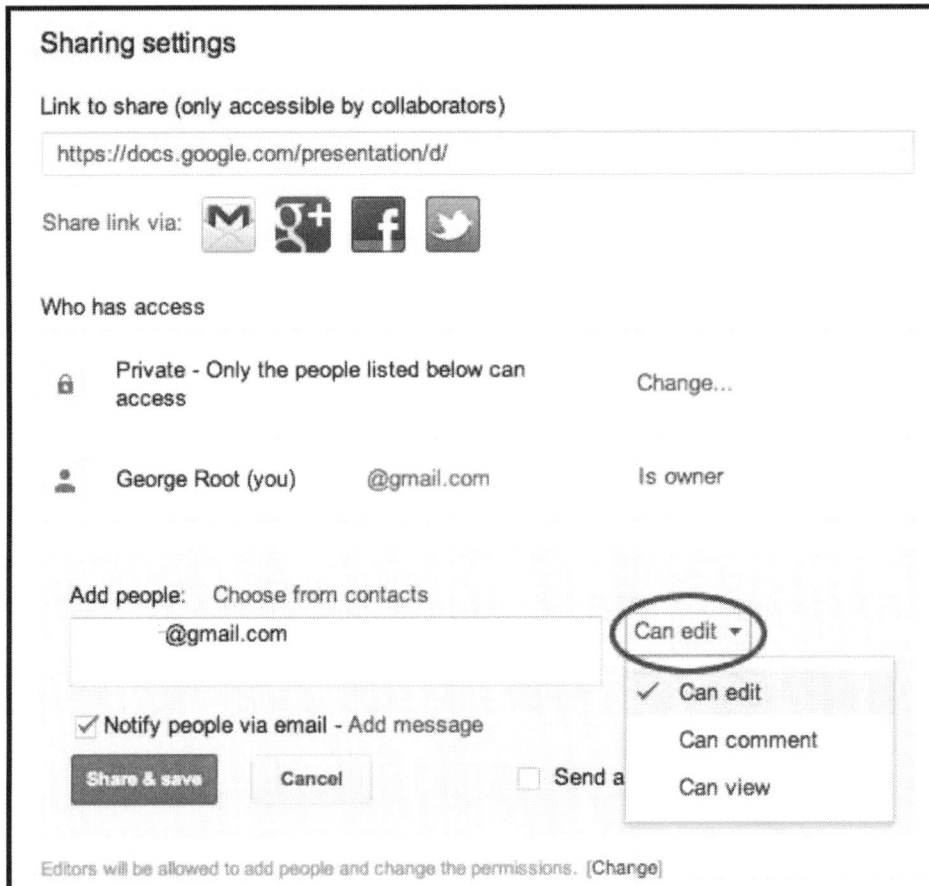

You can select people to share with via Google+, FaceBook, Twitter, or by old fashioned email. In Figure 7.7 I have chosen to share via email by entering the email address (not shown) of the person I want to share the document with. To the right of the person's email address is a drop down menu listing three privileges you can grant to the recipient. You can allow the recipient: to edit the document, or to add a comment on the document but not to edit it, or to view the document but not make any changes to it. In Figure 7.7 I have allowed my collaborator to edit the document.

Be sure the "Notify people via email" box is checked. Once you click the "Share & Save" button, an email message will be sent to the recipient(s) you have chosen. Figure 7.8 shows an example of this email message. All the recipient has to do is click on the file icon in blue, "mySharedDoc" in this case, and the document will open on that person's computer. You will be able to see any changes that person makes if you have the document open at the same time.

Figure 7.8 - The Person You're Sharing With Gets an email Message

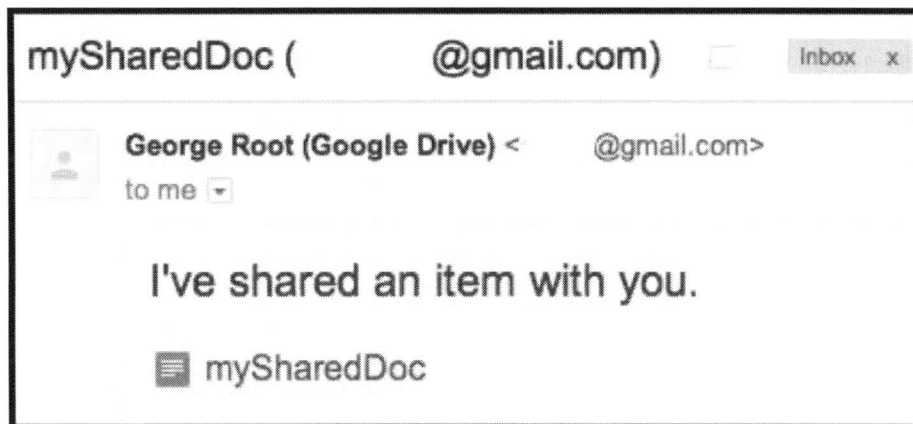

Documents that you have shared will have a "Shared" tag in Google Drive. Want to share a document with more people or remove someone who no longer needs access to the document? Just go to your Drive folder and right-click on the file for which you want to make changes and select "Sharing" from the drop-down menu. This will open the "Sharing Settings" window for that document. This window will look like the one in Figure 7.7 except that it will list all of the people you have shared the document with and the level of access you have granted to each. You can change the access level by clicking on the downward pointing disclosure arrow next to each access granted, "Can Edit" for example. You can remove a person by clicking the "X" next to their name. You can also add more people simply by adding a new email addresses as illustrated in Figure 7.7.

Sharing and collaborating on documents in Chrome is really easy. It takes longer to explain how to do it than it does to actually do it.

7.4 - Creating a Google "Docs" (Word Processor File)

To create a Google Document, open the Google Drive window. If you're using the Chrome Browser go to:

https://drive.google.com/#my-drive

If you have installed the "Black Menu" extension to your Chrome Browser, you can also reach the Google Drive by clicking on the "Black Menu" extension icon and selecting "Drive" from the drop-down menu that appears.

Or, if you are using a Chrome Device simply click on the Google Drive app in the Launcher Bar (see Figure 2.7). In any case, the Drive window will open with a big red "Create" button in the upper left corner - see Figure 7.2. Click on this button and a menu will drop down listing all of the things you can "create" on your Google Drive - see Figure 7.2 again. Just click on the type of new document you want to create - a "Document" in this case.

When you click on the "Create" and then "Document" icons shown in Figure 7.2, a window opens with a new word processing document as illustrated in Figure 7.9:

Figure 7.9 - A New "Docs" Word Processing Document

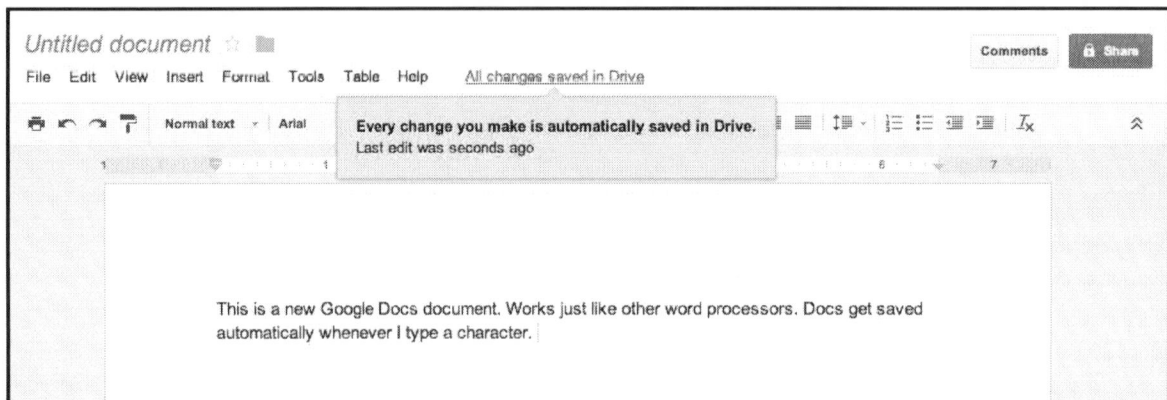

To give this document a name, click on "Untitled document" in the upper-left corner and type a name. By default, this new document is automatically stored in your Drive. If you want it stored in a different folder, click on the folder icon just to the right of the file name in Figure 7.9. This will open a panel like that shown in Figure 7.10.

Figure 7.10 - Select Which Folder to Store Your Document In

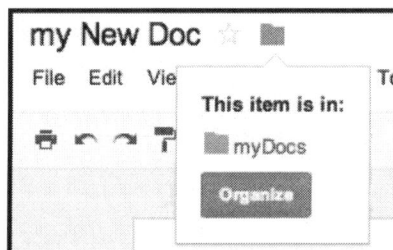

In Figure 7.10 I have already given the document a new name "my New Doc". Click on the blue "Organize" button and a new "Organize" panel will open as illustrated in Figure 7.11. This is where you can select or create a folder in which to store your new document.

Figure 7.11 - You Can Organize Files by Moving Them into a Different Folder

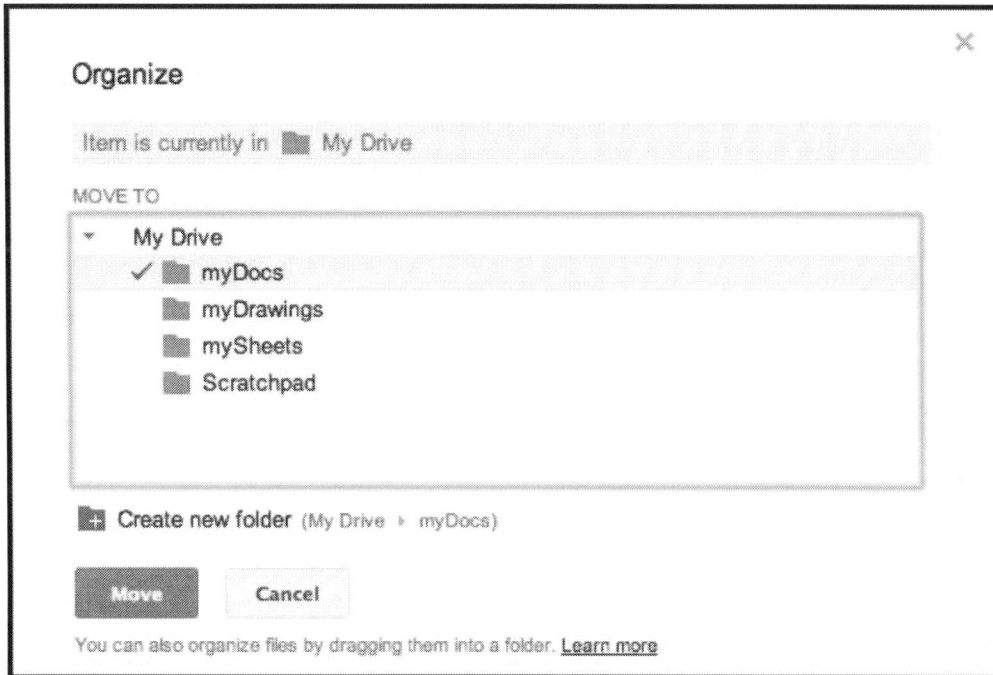

Notice that near the top of this panel it tells you where the file is currently stored: "Item is currently in <Folder> My Drive". You can select which folder you want to move the file to by selecting one of the displayed folders, or you can create a new folder by clicking on the icon just below the main "Move To" menu. You complete the move by clicking on the blue "Move" button.

Also notice that at the very bottom of Figure 7.11, the Chrome dialog tells you that you could accomplish the same thing by simply dragging the file into the desired folder.

When you perform any of these actions, creating or moving files and folders, don't expect instant results. Remember that the action is actually taking place on Google servers somewhere in the cloud. So, you do have to wait patiently while your commands are sent over the internet to Google and the results of those commands are sent back to you.

That's enough to get you started creating and storing Google "Docs". I'm not going to go into any detail on how to actually use the Google "Docs" app. That could be the subject of another book. If you have used any other word processing application like Word on Windows or Pages on Macs, you will find Google Docs to be very similar. You may be surprised to find advanced features such as an equation editor built into "Docs". For most word processing tasks, "Docs" will be more than adequate. If you get stuck, there is a "Help" menu above the work area as illustrated in Figures 7.9 and 7.12. For

"Docs" the menu item "Function List" shown in Figure 7.12 will be missing. You can also go to this site to read all about Google Docs directly from Google:

https://support.google.com/drive/bin/answer.py?hl=en&answer=143206&topic=21008&rd=1

There is "one more thing". There is a nice feature that is available in all of the "Google Docs" apps except Forms and it is so useful I thought I would mention it here. It is named the "Paint Format" tool and it is represented by an icon that looks like a small paint roller just below the "View" menu in Figure 7.9. This tool allows you to copy the formatting of a section of text and then "paint" that formatting onto a different section of text. It doesn't change the text, just its format. To start, select a section of text that is formatted the way you want and then click on the "Paint Format" tool icon. Now drag the cursor across the text to which you want to apply this formatting. When you release the mouse button, the text that you have highlighted will change to the new format you have "painted". If you are going to want to paint the new format onto several different sections of text, start by double clicking on the "Paint Format" tool after you have selected the text whose format you wish to copy. You can then paint the new format onto several different sections of text. When you're done, just click on the "Paint Format" tool again.

You can also use the "Paint Format" tool using keyboard shortcuts. Select the text whose format you want to copy. Type Ctrl+Option+C to copy the formatting. Select the text you want to apply the new formatting to and type Ctrl+Option+V. You can repeat the paste formatting step as many times as you like.

7.5 - Creating Google "Sheets" and "Slides" Documents

Google "Sheets" creates spreadsheets similar to Excel and "Slides" creates slide presentations similar to PowerPoint. The process of creating and storing these documents is identical to the process for creating and storing "Docs" documents as described in section 7.4. The only difference is that in Figure 7.2 you would click on "Spreadsheet" or "Presentation" rather than "Document". If you are familiar with Excel or PowerPoint on your PC, or Numbers or Keynote on your Mac, you already know enough to get started with the corresponding Google apps.

I'm not going to go into any detail on how to actually use the Google "Sheets" or "Slides" apps. That could also be the subject of another book. If you get stuck, there is always a "Help" menu above the work area as illustrated in Figure 7.12.

Figure 7.12 - The "Help" Menu for Google "Sheets"

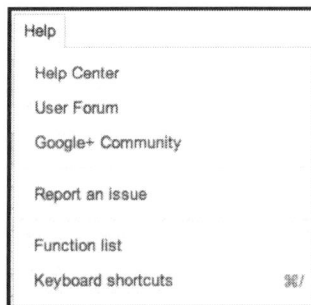

You can also go to this site to read all about Google Sheets directly from Google:

https://support.google.com/drive/bin/answer.py?hl=en&answer=140784&topic=20322&rd=1

You can also go to this site to read all about Google Slides directly from Google:

https://support.google.com/drive/bin/answer.py?hl=en&answer=126127&topic=19431&rd=1

7.6 - Creating a Google "Drawing" Document

I am going to go into a little more detail with Google "Drawings" because there isn't an "Office-like" equivalent that I know of although I'm sure that there are many equivalent drawing programs available for Windows - probably not free however. On Macs, "Pages" has a page layout function that is similar to Google Drawings.

Basically Google "Drawings" creates and edits documents, drawings if you like, containing geometric figures and text. It is ideal for creating org charts or flow diagrams. At this time, these Drawings are limited to 8.5 x 11 inch paper. If this changes in the future, you will find a paper-size menu in the Print Dialog.

To create a new drawing, go to the Google Drive page (read the first few paragraphs of section 7.4 if you don't know how to do this), click on "Create" and select "Drawing" in the drop down menu. You will now have a blank - 8.5 by 11 inch - canvas. As an example, Figure 7.13 illustrates the broad range of line styles you can create. There are equally large choices for shapes. You can also insert images - your company logo for example - "Word Art", and normal text into your drawings. Figure 7.14 shows an example of the type of drawing you can create in just a few minutes.

Figure 7.13 - A Wide Range of Shapes and Line Styles is Available

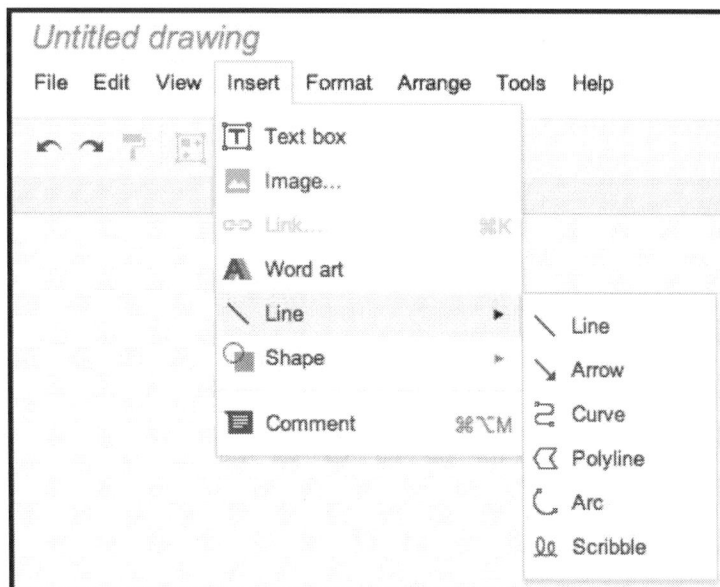

Figure 7.14 - A Google Drawing Created in Just a Few Minutes

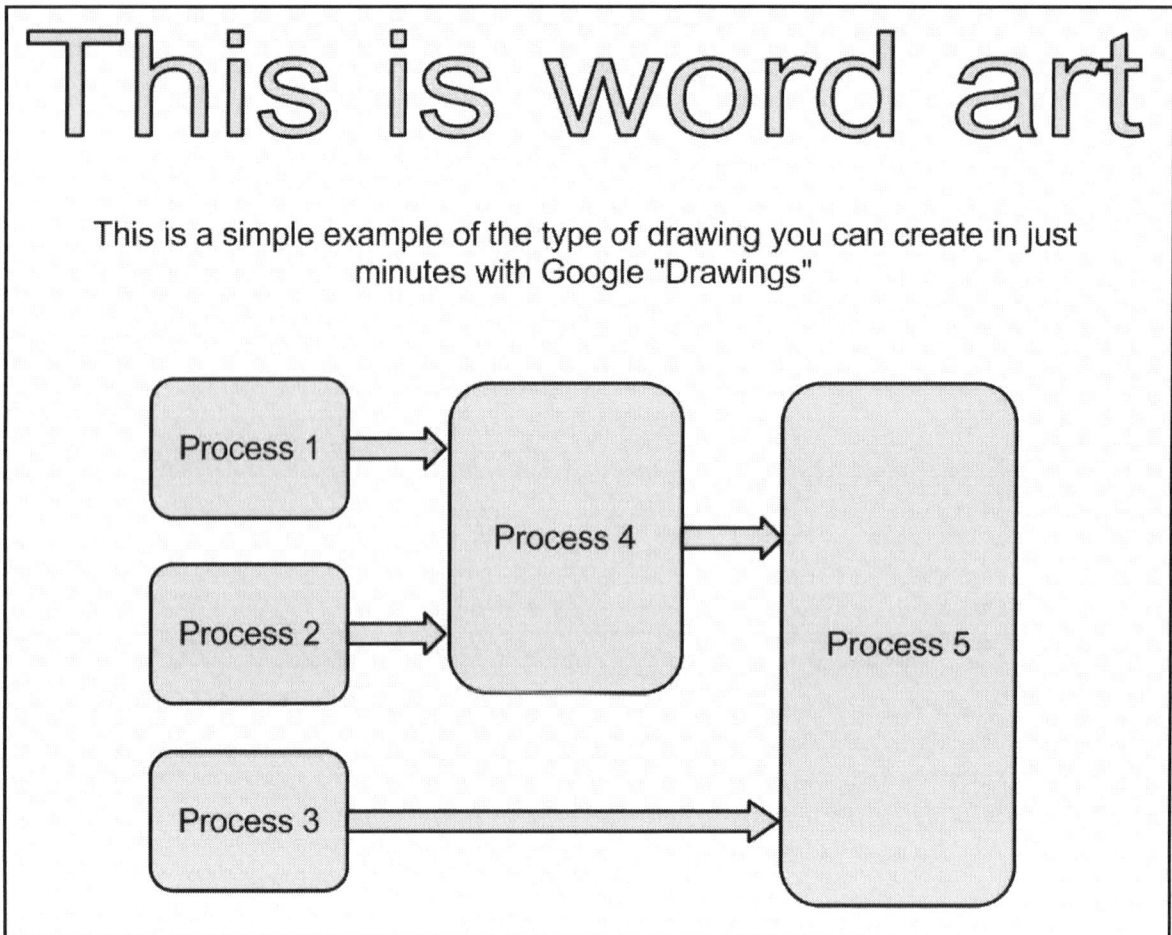

You can also include your Drawings in Google Docs, Sheets, and Slides documents. First, create your Drawing in the Drawing app. You can then copy the entire Drawing or a part of it to the "Web Clipboard". Notice that this is not the clipboard on your computer. If you do a "Copy" from the Edit menu, what you have copied will go onto the clipboard on your personal computer. But Google needs it to be accessible on the web so that it can perform the paste operation later. So, you use the "Web Clipboard" instead of the personal computer one. Figure 7.15 illustrates this Copy action.

Figure 7.15 - Use the Web Clipboard to Copy Your Drawing

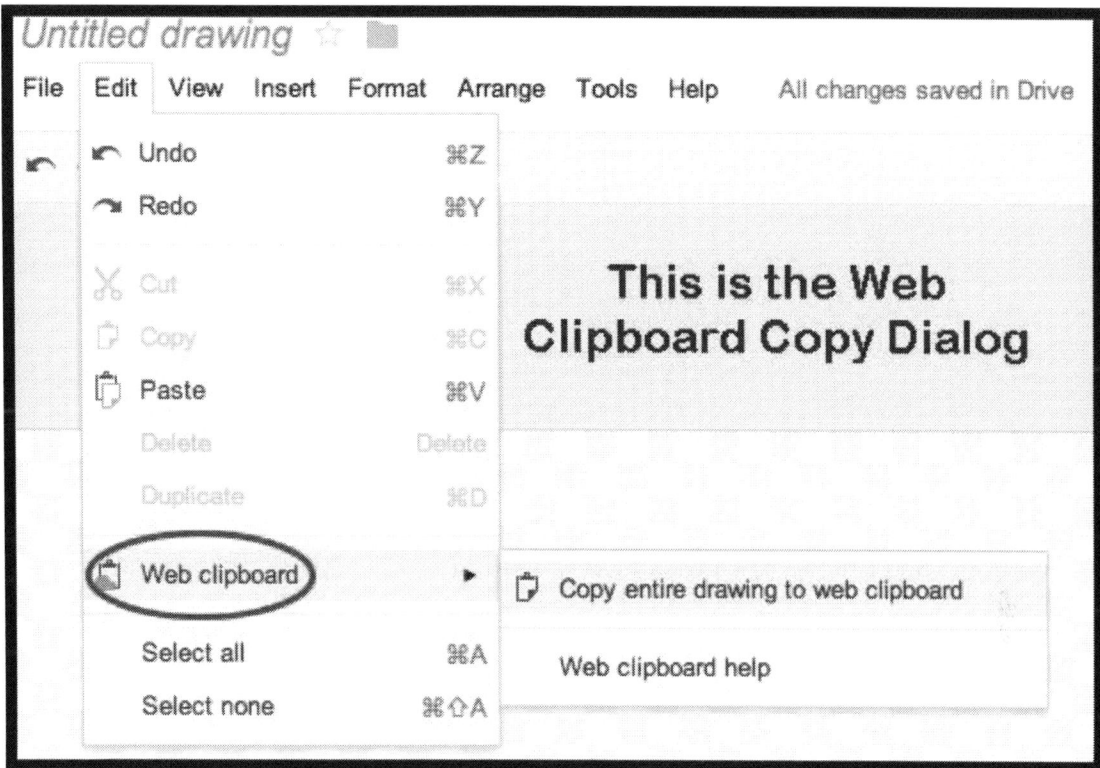

Notice in Figure 7.15 I have chosen "Web Clipboard" from the Edit Menu in the Drawing app rather than the ordinary "Copy" item shown dimmed out higher up. Be sure not to use Ctrl+C as a shortcut to this Web Clipboard action. Now that you have copied your Drawing onto the Web Clipboard, open the document you want to paste it into. Place an insertion point and select "Web Clipboard" > "Drawing". This will insert your drawing from the Drawing app into the document you are creating using Docs, Sheets, or Slides. This is illustrated in Figure 7.16. Notice that in Figure 7.16 I did not select "Paste" from the edit menu.

Figure 7.16 - Use the Web Clipboard to Paste Your Drawing

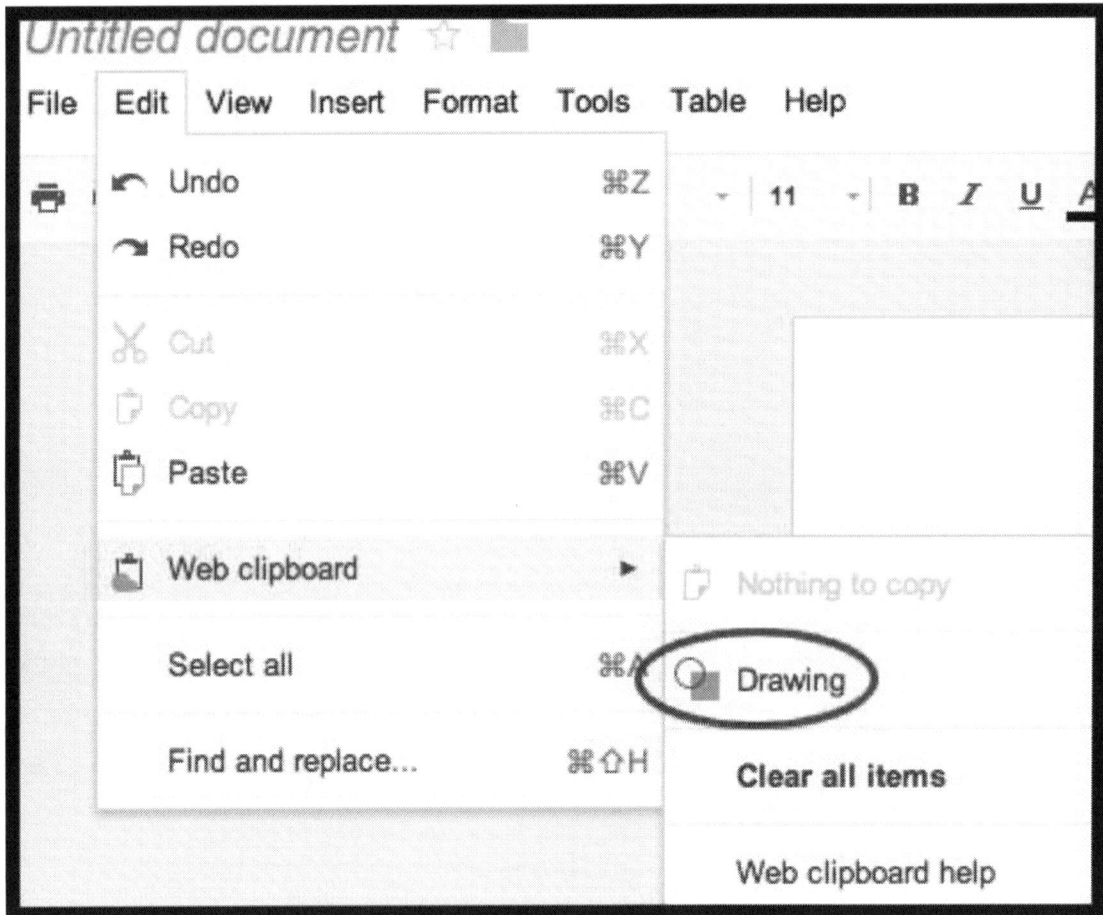

If the drawing you want to include in your Docs, Sheets, or Slides document is simple, you can also create it right in the Docs, Sheets, or Slides document itself. Just click on the "Insert" menu in the toolbar and select "Drawing" from the drop-down menu that appears. This will bring up a blank canvas where you can create your drawing right in the document.

There is another way to create a drawing in the Drawing app and then copy-and-paste it into a Docs, Slides or Sheets document: Create your Drawing in the Drawing app as usual. Then use your screen capture app to "take a picture" of that drawing. You can then insert this "image" into your Docs, Slides or Sheets document by selecting "Insert" > "Image".

On your Chrome Device, you can take a screen shot by holding down Ctrl+Shift and hitting the window switcher button (the one that looks like a deck of cards = F5 on a PC keyboard) and then drawing a rectangle around the entire Drawing or any part of it on your screen. Using the Chrome Browser on a Mac, you can accomplish the exact same thing by holding down Cmd+Shift and hitting the number "4" key. Use the resulting cross-hairs cursor to draw a rectangle around the Drawing on your screen. There is undoubtedly a similar capability in Windows, but I'm not familiar with it.

7.7 - Creating a Google "Forms" Document

Google "Forms" is an interesting type of document. You may have received one yourself lately. It seems to be popular right now for businesses to send out questionnaires to see "how are we doing". You rate various aspects of the business and then send the filled out form back to the company. Google Forms let you do this same type of thing with the added benefit that it will also tally up the results for you and present those results as a Sheets spreadsheet document.

For example, my local bike club is sponsoring a charity ride and I want to see how many people are going to participate, and if they are, how far they plan to ride and so forth. So I have created a simple Forms document as illustrated in Figure 7.17:

Figure 7.17 - A Simple Forms Document Received via eMail

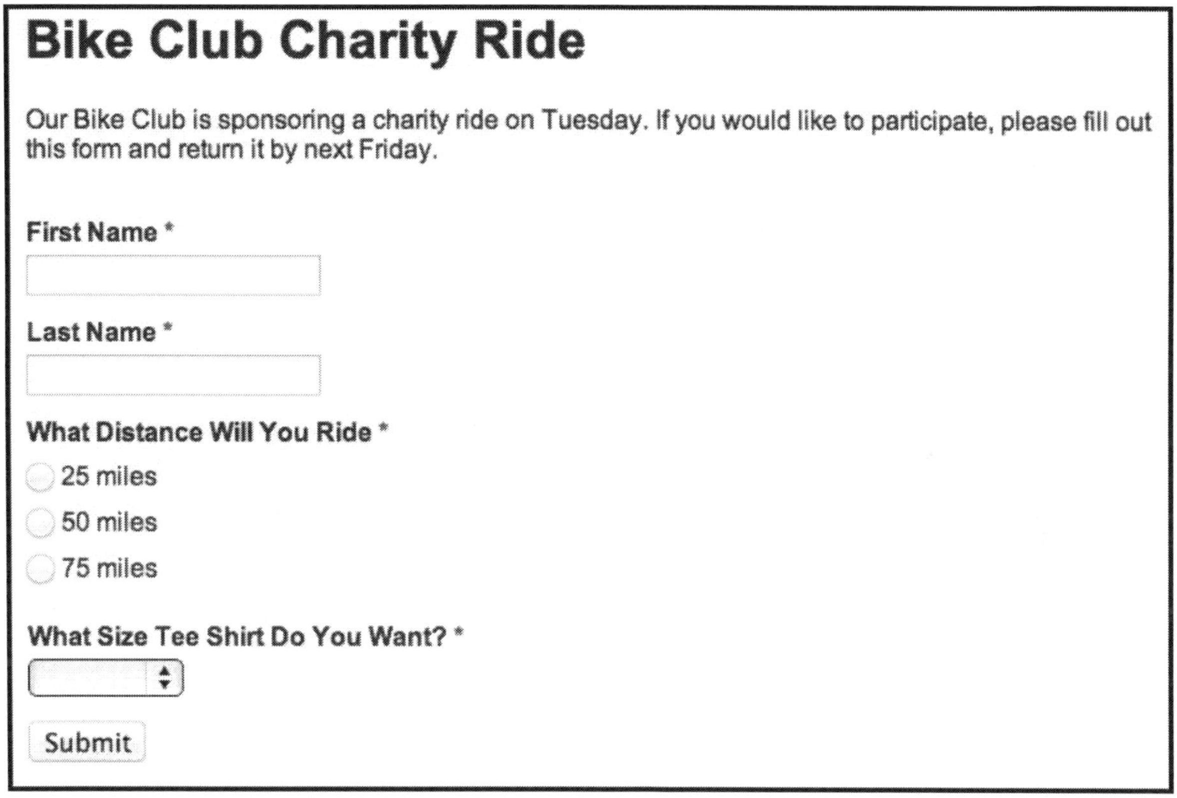

Bike Club Charity Ride

Our Bike Club is sponsoring a charity ride on Tuesday. If you would like to participate, please fill out this form and return it by next Friday.

First Name *

Last Name *

What Distance Will You Ride *

○ 25 miles

○ 50 miles

○ 75 miles

What Size Tee Shirt Do You Want? *

Submit

I'm not going to describe the steps I took to create this form, but I will tell you that it was so simple, it didn't take more than 2 minutes. I'm going to give you a link to the Google tutorial on how to create and use forms so you can see just how simple it really is.

When I finished creating my form, I sent it out via email. I could have sent it to a Google Group, for example my Bike Club's Google Group. There isn't really a bike club so I just sent it to myself as an illustration. Figure 7.17 is actually what I received in the email message. And I could have forwarded this email to other friends who might be interested. I could have distributed the form via Google+, FaceBook, or Twitter. So it isn't difficult to create the form nor to give it wide distribution.

Once the recipients fill out and return, "Submit", the forms, Google generates a summary of responses as illustrated in Figure 7.18. I have edited out some of the less interesting stuff such as the names of responders (which were all fake anyway) so as to save space on the page.

Figure 7.18 - Edited Summary of Form Responses

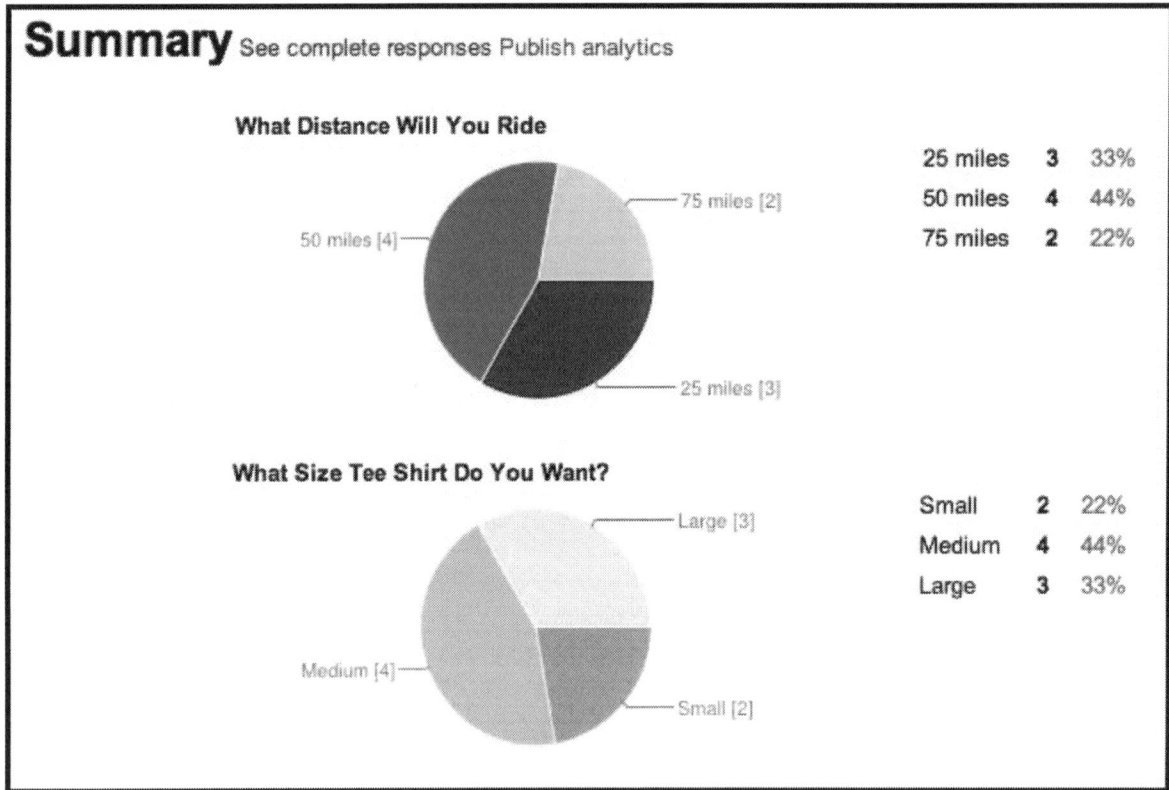

In addition to this summary of responses - I need 4 medium tee shirts for example - Google also creates a Sheets spreadsheet that contains all of the individual responses. Such a spreadsheet is illustrated in Figure 7.19.

Figure 7.19 - "Sheets" Spreadsheet Containing All the Responses

Timestamp	What Distance Will You Ride	What Size Tee Shirt Do You Want?	First Name	Last Name
2/24/2013 18:12:07	50 miles	Small	Rider	Two
2/24/2013 18:13:15	75 miles	Small	Rider	Five
2/24/2013 18:09:56	25 miles	Medium	Rider	One
2/24/2013 18:12:52	50 miles	Medium	Rider	Four
2/24/2013 18:13:35	25 miles	Medium	Rider	Six
2/24/2013 18:12:34	75 miles	Large	Rider	Three
2/24/2013 18:13:55	50 miles	Large	Rider	Seven

Because this is a full fledged spreadsheet it can be modified as any other spreadsheet. For example, I have sorted the Sheet illustrated in Figure 7.19 based on Tee Shirt Size so that I can see which riders get each size.

So, this illustrates a lot of things you can do quite easily with Google Forms. You can read all about how to create and use Google Forms directly from Google by going here:

http://support.google.com/drive/bin/answer.py?hl=en&answer=87809

8 - Using Google Calendar

8.1 - Overview of the Google Calendar Window

Google Calendar is a real powerhouse with so many features that it is difficult even to summarize all of them. You can, of course, enter events - single instance or repeating. You can schedule meetings and invite participants - Google Calendar will help you find a time when everyone is available. Google Calendar can remind you of important events via email or SMS text message. You can have multiple calendars - one for business and one for personal events, for example. You can share your calendars with other family members or people with whom you work. To get started, let's look at the Calendar window as illustrated in Figure 8.1:

Figure 8.1 - The Main Google Calendar Window

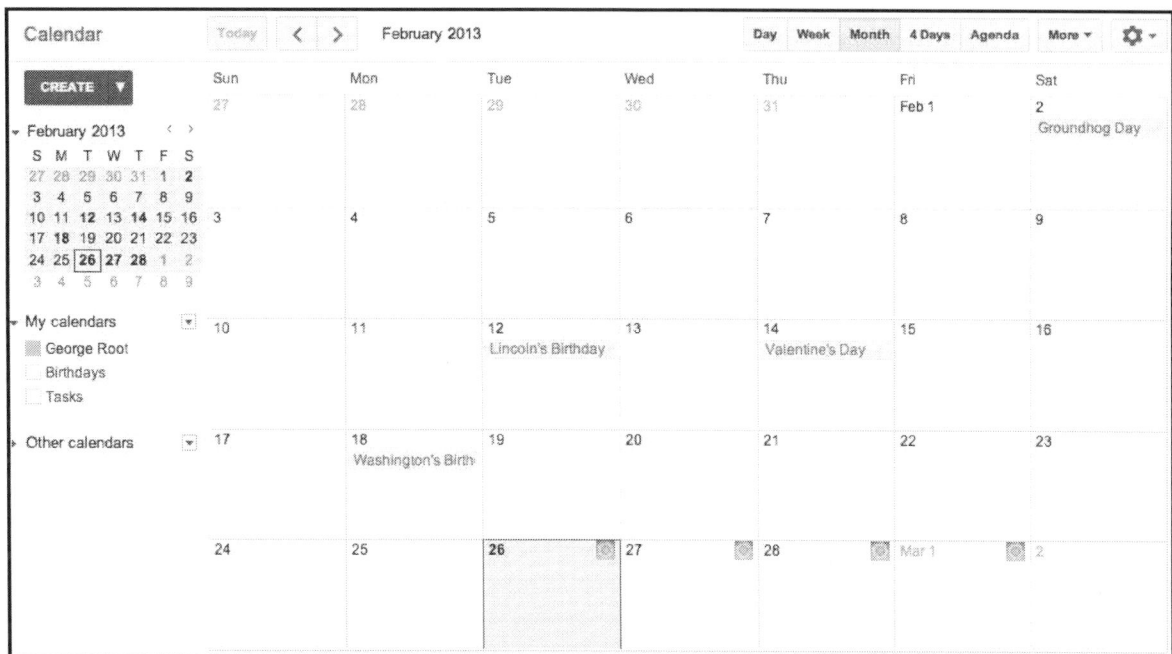

There are three main areas of the Calendar window that I will be discussing:

1) In the upper right corner is a tab bar where you can choose different calendar views. To the right of this tab bar is the "Gear Icon" which will reveal a drop-down menu where you can, among other things, open the Calendar Settings window.

2) In the upper left corner of the Calendar window is the big red "Create" button you should be familiar with by now. This is actually a two part button. The left hand portion of this button, labeled "Create", allows you to create a new calendar event (see section 8.4) and control every aspect of this event. The right hand portion of this button, identified only with a downward pointing disclosure triangle, opens a "Quick Create" pane where you can create a "short form" calendar event. This is also explained in section 8.4.

3) The third area of interest is the main Calendar window itself. This is where all of your events appear. You can view these events in several different formats.

8.2 - Choose the Format of the Google Calendar Window

Figure 8.1 shows the default Calendar "Month" view. You can change views by clicking on the row of tabs in the upper right corner of the window shown in Figure 8.1. The "Day", "Week", and "Month" views are pretty self explanatory. You can choose which day, Saturday, Sunday, or Monday, the "week" starts on in Calendar Settings. The "4 Days" view shows hourly schedules for the next four days. I prefer the "Agenda" view illustrated in Figure 8.2. The Agenda view shows a list of upcoming events in chronological order. Calendar adds a weather forecast for the next four days to the Agenda view.

Figure 8.2 - Google Calendar in "Agenda" View

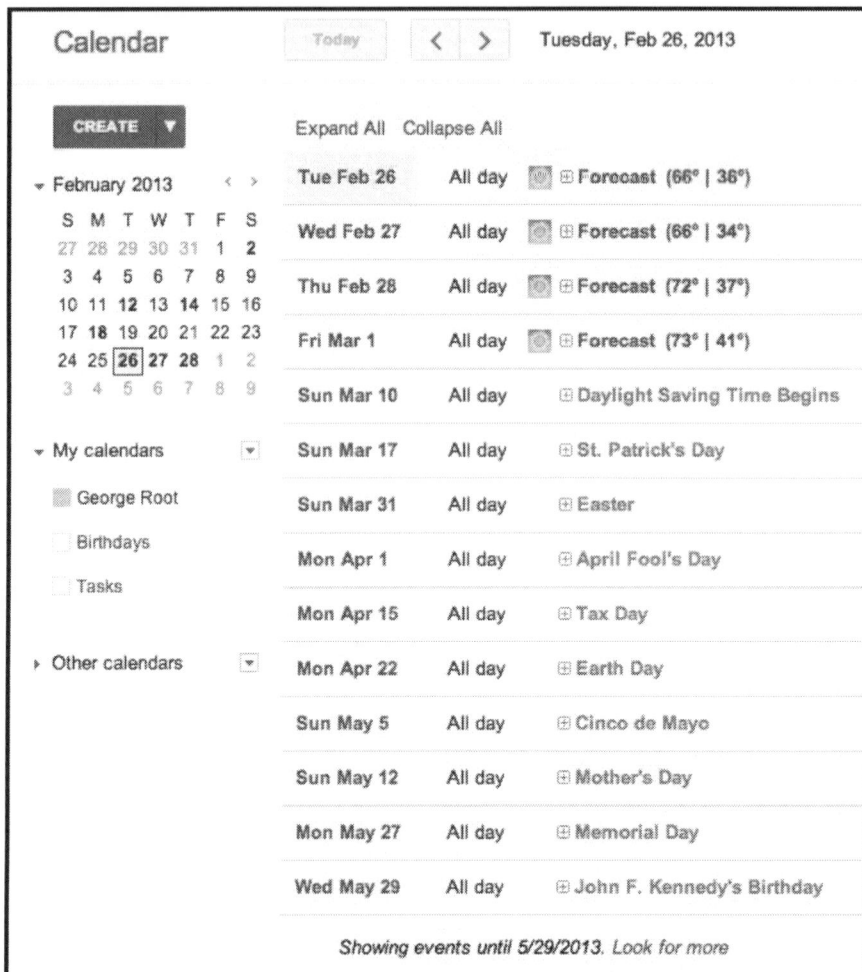

8.3 - Set Up "Settings" for Your Google Calendar

The "Gear Icon" in the upper right corner of the Calendar window drops down a menu where you can select several things including "Settings" for your Calendar app. This is illustrated in Figure 8.3:

Figure 8.3 - The "Gear Icon" Takes You to Calendar Settings

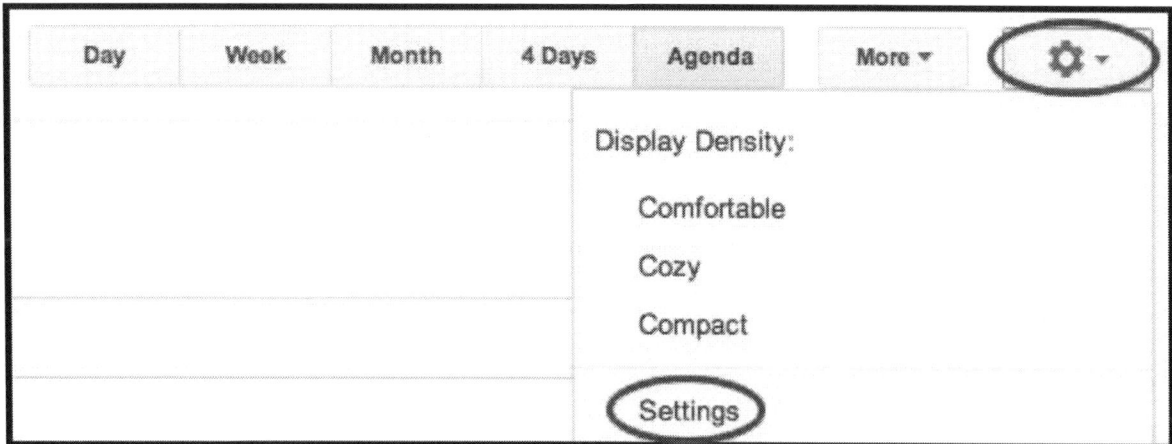

There are dozens and dozens of different settings that you can select to customize exactly how your Calendar looks and works. In order to organize all of the possible Calendar settings, Google has divided them up into four tabs as illustrated in Figure 8.4:

Figure 8.4 - There are Four Tabs of Calendar Settings

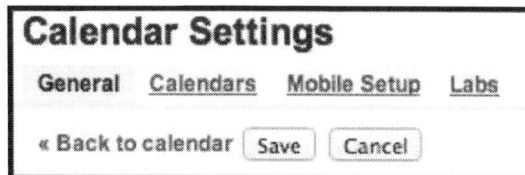

Under the "General" Settings tab you will find stuff like: Date and Time format, what day the "week" starts on, what view to use as the default, and others. The two settings at the bottom of this list might be useful to you. One displays "Tips" on using Calendar and the other enables keyboard shortcuts that you might like to use.

Under the "Calendars" settings tab you will find a list of all your calendars with checkboxes to share your calendars and set up notifications and reminders for your events. You can subscribe and un-subscribe to other calendars - import and export calendars - and create new calendars here.

Under the "Mobile Setup" tab you can enter a mobile phone number where you would like SMS text messages sent to notify you of Calendar events. You can also set up syncing of your Google Calendar with your Android or iPhone mobile.

Google "Labs" is where Google engineers try out new ideas before releasing them in a standard version of Chrome. So, the "Labs" tab in Calendar Settings shows what things Google is thinking about including in a future release of Calendar. Everything here is disabled by default, but you can choose to enable any or all of them. Be aware that some bugs may still be running around in the "Labs" tab (that's why Google wants you to try out these things). A couple of Labs extras that caught my eye are: "Year View" for planning months in advance; "Jump to Date" to go to a date in the future or past; "World Clock" - if you travel a lot this might be very handy.

8.4 - Creating Google Calendar Events

Clicking on the left side of the red Create button in the upper left corner of the Calendar window will open a pane where you can specify every detail of a new Calendar event. This is illustrated in Figure 8.5:

Figure 8.5 - Creating a New Calendar Event

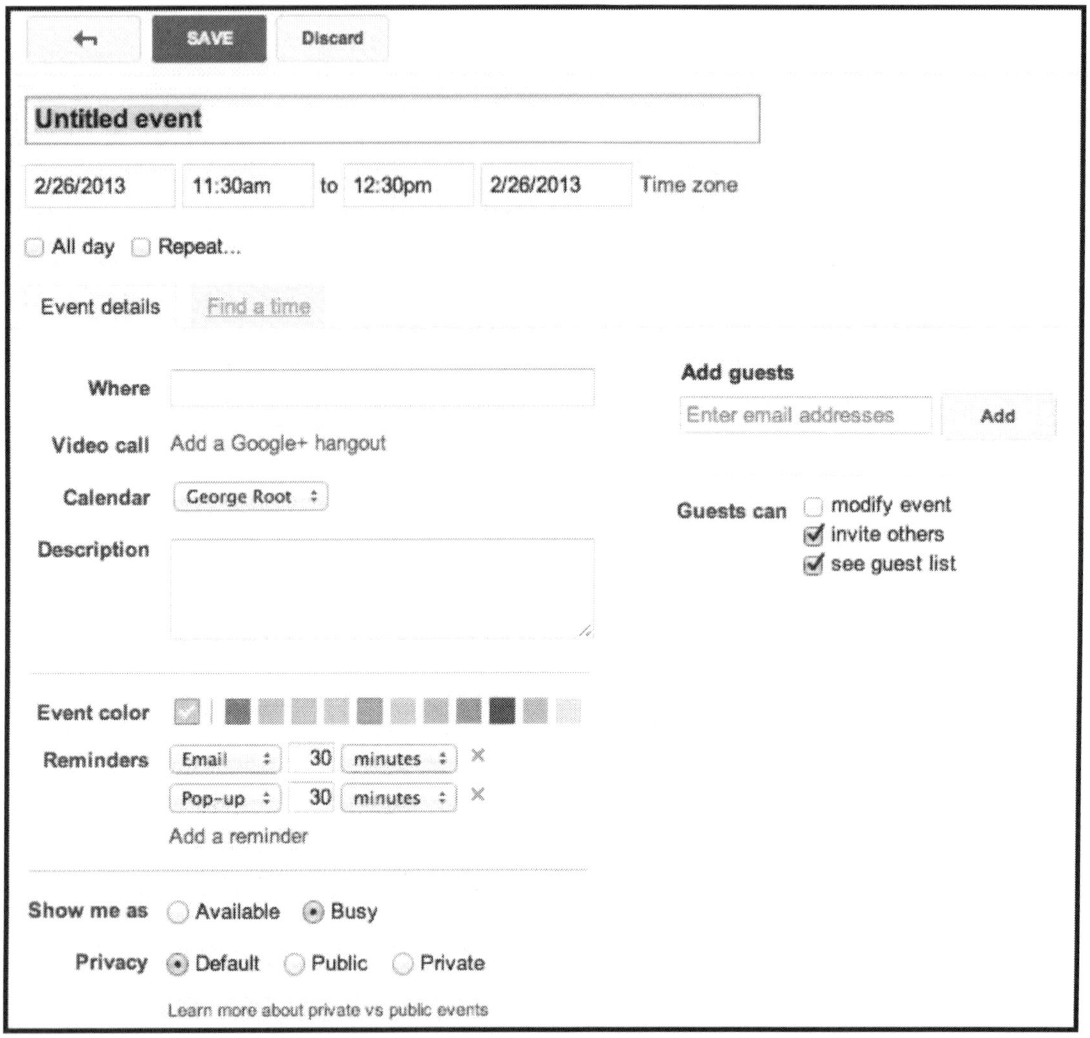

For a simple event, all you need do is give the event a name and enter a time and date. You can make the event repeating or all day. Repeating events have a wide range of repeat intervals to choose from: daily, on specific days, M-F only, weekly, etc.

For more complex events such as business meetings or birthday parties, you can choose people to invite and Calendar will send them invitations. If the other participants also share their Google Calendars with you, Calendar will even help you find a time when all your chosen participants are available.

If you are creating a simple event, you may not need all of the options available in the full "Create" window. In this case, click on the right side of the red Create button - on the downward pointing disclosure triangle shown in Figure 8.2. This opens a simpler way to create an event as illustrated in Figure 8.6:

Figure 8.6 - Creating a Simple Calendar Event

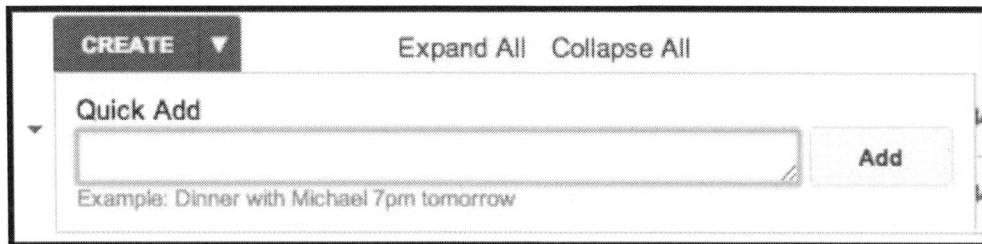

You just type your event description using "natural language". The example Google gives is "Dinner with Michael at 7pm tomorrow". You can say things like "on Thursday" to schedule the event for next Thursday. If you type something that Google doesn't understand, Calendar opens the full event creation window as shown in Figure 8.5 where you can clarify what you tried to say.

That's enough to get you started. Poke around in Calendar and you will find a lot of stuff that I haven't mentioned. You can also go here to read the latest from Google:

http://support.google.com/calendar/?hl=en

9 - Using Gmail & Contacts

Setting up and using Gmail is a very large topic - so large that entire books can be, and have been, written about it. In this section I will try to cover the "high points" - just enough to get you started and then, following the technique I have used in previous sections, I will give you a link to the Google support page where you will be able to read all about Gmail.

In Mac OS X, the "Contacts" app is separate from the "Mail" app. And, the Mail app keeps its own list of email addresses for people with whom you have exchanged email messages. This leads to the unfortunate situation where the user can have two different email addresses for the same person - one from the Contacts app and a different one from the Mail app. Google avoids this problem by eliminating the separate "Contacts" app. There is one, and only one, list of Contacts in Chrome and that is the one maintained by Gmail. That's why we are discussing both Gmail and Contacts together in this section.

9.1 - Getting to Know Gmail

Figure 9.1 is an illustration of one way to set up your Gmail window. There is a lot to see in this figure. First, notice that, since this is a Google service, we have the Google "Black Bar" across the top of the figure. This allows quick access to other Google services.

Figure 9.1 - One Way to Set Up Your Gmail Window

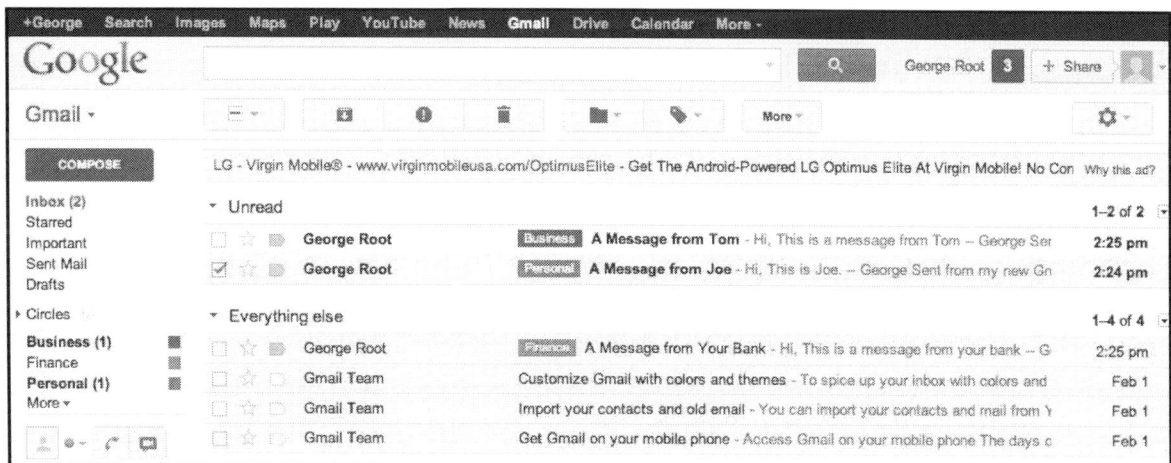

The Gmail Search Box:

Just below the "Black Bar" is a Google search box. In this case, you will be searching your email messages. So, for example, if I were to enter "Tom" in the search box, Google would find all the messages that contain "Tom".

There are dozens of ways to narrow your Gmail searches. You might want to do this if your original, simple search turned up too many matches. You just type these search-narrowing terms, called operators, before typing what you are searching for. For example, here are a few operators you can use to narrow your search:

from:
example = from:Joe = find messages <u>from</u> Joe

to:
example = to:Joe = find messages <u>to</u> Joe

subject:
example = subject:lunch = find messages with the word "lunch" in the Subject line

in:anywhere
example = in:anywhere Joe = search, including Trash and Spam, for Joe

newer_than:2d
example = newer_than:2d Joe = find messages newer than 2 days old containing Joe

You can also concatenate search operators: "newer_than:2d from:joe" will find messages newer than 2 days ago sent by Joe.

The Row of Icons:

Below the Google Search box is a row of icons shown in more detail in Figure 9.2. These icons appear once at least one message is selected. To select a message, click in the small box to the left of the message as illustrated with the second message in Figure 9.1. Selected messages will be highlighted in yellow. The row of icons provides various actions you can perform on selected messages. I have shown these buttons as icons since this is the default behavior. However, if you prefer, you can have these buttons labeled with text rather than icons. You can change the way these buttons are labeled in General Settings. Refer to section 9.3 for more information about Gmail Settings.

Figure 9.2 - The Row of Icons in the Gmail Window

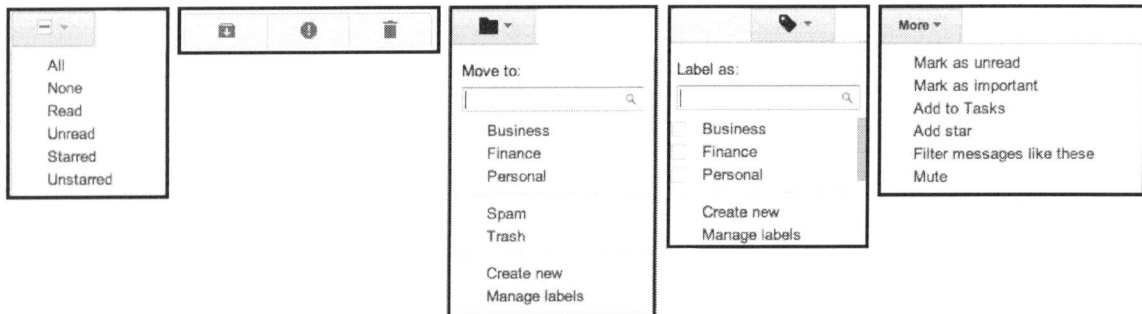

The first icon that looks like a "-" allows you to select various sets of messages from the drop down menu, for example all "Unread" messages. This icon will always be there even if no messages are selected.

The next set of three icons appear when a message is selected. They perform their actions immediately when they are clicked and don't have drop down menus.

The first of these three - it looks like a box with a downward pointing arrow - sends selected messages to the "Archives". Archived messages are not deleted, but they are removed from your inbox. They are moved into your "All Mail" label where you can still find them. To reveal your "All Mail" label, click on the "More" button shown near the lower left corner of Figure 9.1. Search results will include archived messages.

The middle icon in the triptych is the "Report as Spam" button. Google provides excellent spam filtering. Messages that Google considers to be spam never reach your inbox. They are automatically labeled as "Spam" and they are put into your "Spam" folder where you can still find them if you want to. One of the reasons Google spam filtering is so good is that users help define what is spam by selecting a message that is spam and then clicking on this button. Note that there are two types of junk mail. Advertising mail that you receive from companies you have done business with is annoying, but it isn't spam. Spam comes from senders you don't know and is often, better yet always, intended to get you to do something that will be bad for you - like clicking on a link to take you "to your bank" where you can enter your account details. Businesses send junk mail. Hackers and crooks send spam.

The last icon in the triptych is the "Delete" button. Select one or more messages and click this icon to delete those messages. Deleted messages are sent to the Trash folder where they remain for about 30 days after which time they are really deleted. You can find your Trash mailbox by clicking the "More" button shown near the lower left corner of Figure 9.1. Search results will include Deleted messages until they are really deleted after 30 days.

You can retrieve deleted messages from the "Trash" by clicking on the "Trash" mailbox and selecting the message you want to retrieve. When you select the message, a drop down menu will appear from which you select "Move" and then "Inbox". Remember, after 30 days messages cannot be retrieved.

You can immediately, and permanently delete a message in your Trash mailbox by: Click on the "Trash" mailbox. Check the box next to the message you want to immediately delete. Click the "Delete Forever" button.

You have to be careful when deleting a message from a conversation. If you select a message from a conversation and click the "Delete" icon, the entire conversation will be deleted. If you only want to delete that one message: Select the message by checking the box next to it. Click the downward pointing disclosure triangle next to "Reply" and select "Delete this message".

The next icon in Figure 9.2 - it looks like a folder with a downward pointing disclosure triangle next to it - is the "Move to" icon. Select a message and click on this icon. A drop down menu will list all of the places you can "Move" the selected message(s) to. Just click on the one you want and the message will be moved to that mailbox. The available mailboxes include the system provided "Spam" and

"Trash" mailboxes plus any that you have created by defining a "label" as I will describe next. In the example shown in Figure 9.2, I have defined the labels "Business", "Finance", and "Personal".

The next icon in Figure 9.2 - it looks like a luggage tag - allows you to attach labels to messages and to define and manage your labels. I'm going to defer a more thorough discussion of labels and mailboxes until section 9.2. It's a big and sometimes confusing topic and it needs more space than available here.

Finally, the last icon in Figure 9.2 titled "More" opens a drop down menu with several actions you can apply to selected messages. For example, if you are reading a message but want to keep it labeled "Unread" you can click on "More" and then "Mark as unread". The menu item titled "Filter messages like these" is important and will also be discussed in section 9.2.

At the far right of the row containing all these icons is another one that looks like a gear and it is in fact called the "Gear" icon. Clicking this icon will drop down a menu with a few items of which the two most important are: "Settings" and "Help". There are literally dozens of Gmail settings and they will be the topic of section 9.3.

The Gmail Sidebar:

Returning now to the illustration of the Gmail window shown in Figure 9.1, the left sidebar has a big red "Compose" button at the top. Click this to start a new message. Below "Compose" is a list of your mailboxes. Clicking on one of these mailboxes will show you the subset of all your messages that have been assigned to that mailbox. Nearly all of your incoming messages will arrive in your Inbox and this is probably where you will spend most of your time. Messages that do not appear in your InBox are Spam messages, and messages you have filtered out to "Skip the Inbox". This will be discussed in section 9.2.

The Advertisement:

Google provides dozens of services like Gmail to you for "free". Well, not entirely free. You will often find an advertisement tucked away in the Google service window you are using. In Figure 9.1, the ad is for an LG-Virgin Mobile™ phone. It's a small price to pay to avoid having to actually pay in cash.

The Main Message Pane:

We have finally arrived at the main reason for having Gmail - the messages. The message area illustrated in Figure 9.1 has a couple of features worth noting. First, there are several different ways that you can have your messages organized in this window. I have chosen to display:

Unread First: As you can see in Figure 9.1, all the messages I have not yet read are listed in the first section and then "Everything Else" messages are listed in the following section. Your other options for arranging your messages are:

Classic Inbox: Basically all your messages are arranged chronologically and they stay in your Inbox unless you move them somewhere else. Messages you have read are grayed out and unread ones are shown in bold.

Important First: Google tries to guess which messages you consider important based on how you have treated previous, similar messages. For example, if you always open and reply to messages from Tom, Google will mark subsequent messages from Tom as "Important". You can also label a message as "Important" by clicking on the "arrow" icon to the left of the message sender's name. In Figure 9.1 there are three messages that have been classified as "Important". They have their "arrows" filled in in yellow. There are also three un-important messages with hollow, unfilled, arrows. If Google mistakenly identifies a message either as or as-not Important, you can correct that assignment by clicking on the arrow. This will train Google to correctly classify similar messages in the future.

With an "Important First" Inbox you will have two sections: all messages marked as "Important" and "Everything Else".

Starred First: Each message has a hollow, un-filled star to the left of the sender's name. You "star" the message by clicking on this icon which fills in the star with a color - yellow is the default color. You can use stars in any way you like. For example, when you read a message you might decide that you will want to come back to that message when you have more time to reply. Click the star. You can find your starred messages by clicking on the "Starred" mailbox in the left sidebar. Or, if you have chosen the "Starred First" Inbox style, you will find two sections: "Starred" messages and "Everything Else"

Priority Inbox: With the "Priority Inbox" you will have three sections: The first section will contain all Important and Unread messages. The second section will contain all Starred messages. The last section will contain "Everything Else".

Message Labels:

Some of the messages illustrated in Figure 9.1 have "labels" attached to them. There is a red "Business" label, a blue "Personal" label and a green "Financial" label. The next section will tell you more than you really wanted to know about labels.

9.2 - Labels, Mailboxes, and Filters

One of the questions I had when coming to Gmail from OS X Mail was "where are the folders?" I was accustomed to setting up "rules" that would sort my incoming mail into various folders. Each message could reside in only one folder. This sometimes led to confusion. This message is from my business bank. Should I put it in the "Business" folder or the "Financial" folder or perhaps into the "Tax Related" folder. Well, Google has eliminated this problem in Gmail by doing away with folders (sort of) and introducing "Labels" instead. You can define any labels you want to use. A message can have any number of labels attached to it. So, in my previous "message from the bank" quandary, the Gmail solution is simple: assign all three labels to the bank's message. Now I can find that message by clicking on the "Business" label or the "Financial" label or the "Tax Related" label. The message itself stays in my Inbox (unless I move it somewhere else), but the labels attached to it allow me to find it in any of the classifications (labels) I have attached to it.

9.2.1 - Labels:

You can create as many labels as you like, although a very large number of labels might be difficult to manage. There are two ways to create a new label:

Create a New Label – Method 1:

- Select a message that you want to label
- Click on the "Labels" icon (second from the right) in the icon bar illustrated in Figure 9.2
- Click on "Create New"
- Give the new label a name.

Create a New Label – Method 2:

- Click on the "Gear" icon
- Select "Settings" from the drop down menu
- Select the "Labels" tab
- Click on "Create New Label" near the bottom of the list
- Give the new label a name.

When you create a new label, a new "mailbox" appears in the left sidebar of the Gmail window. You can see all the messages that have been assigned that label by clicking on that "mailbox". Note: the actual messages are still in your Inbox. Clicking on one of these "mailboxes" simply finds all messages with that label.

Newly created labels are a dull gray. To add color, hover the cursor over the name of the mailbox associated with the new label and then click on the downward pointing disclosure triangle that appears. This will open a pane as illustrated in Figure 9.3:

Figure 9.3 - You Can Assign a Color to a New Label

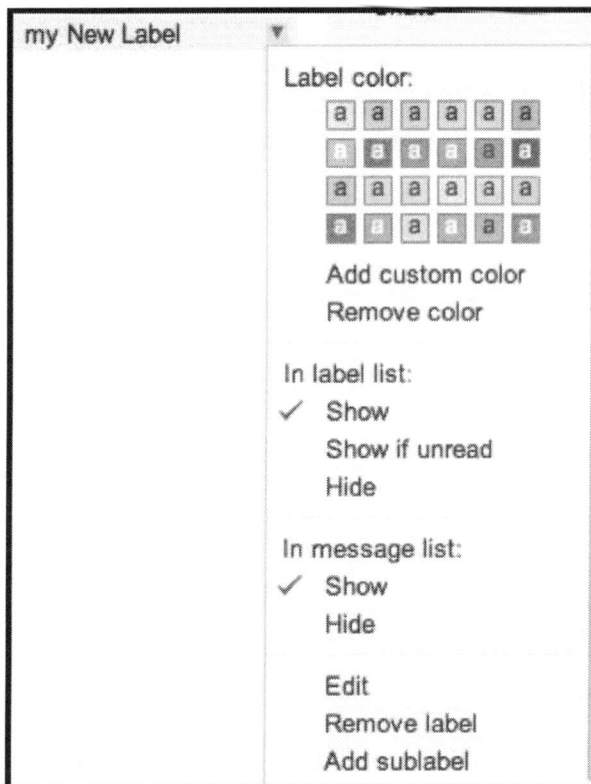

Just click on the desired color, or you can add a custom color if you like.

To apply a label to a message, select the message by clicking the empty box to the left of the sender's name. Now click the "Label as" icon shown in Figure 9.2. Select any labels you want to apply to the message and then click apply.

9.2.2 - Mailboxes:

As I mentioned in section 9.2.1, when you create a new label, you also create a new mailbox. This new mailbox appears in the left sidebar of the Gmail window. It has the same name as the label. This "mailbox" is actually two things at the same time. First, it is a shortcut for selecting all messages with that label. If I click on the "Finance" mailbox in the left sidebar of Figure 9.1, the Inbox will re-populate with only those messages with the "Finance" label. I can return to the full Inbox by clicking on the "Inbox" label at the top of the list of mailboxes in Figure 9.1. But, the "mailboxes" listed in the left sidebar are also actual mailboxes. You can move messages into these mailboxes:

- Select a message
- Click on the "Move to" icon in the icon strip shown in Figure 9.2
- Click on the name of the mailbox you want to move the message into.
- The message will disappear from your Inbox and re-appear in the labeled mailbox.

You can also just drag a message to the desired mailbox. This will simultaneously apply that label to the message.

So, you can remove messages from your Inbox in this way. You can also put them back into the Inbox.

- Click on the Mailbox that contains the message you want to move back into your Inbox
- Select the message you want to move by clicking in the box to the left of the sender's name
- Click on the "Move to" icon in the icon strip shown in Figure 9.2
- Click on the Inbox.
- The message will re-appear in your Inbox. It will also appear to remain in the labeled Mailbox just as before you made any moves.

9.2.3 - Filters:

It would be tiresome if you had to assign labels to messages by hand. Gmail provides "Filters" to do the work for you. A Filter consists of two parts: the Filter part - which messages to act upon - and the action part - what actions to perform on the selected messages.

To create a new Filter, start by selecting a message that has the characteristics you are trying to filter for. For example, if you have set up a "Finances" label, you might want to assign that label to any messages from your bank. So, in this case, select any message from your bank. Now, go to the "More" icon illustrated in Figure 9.2 and select "Filter messages like this". This will open the "Create Filter" pane as illustrated in Figure 9.4:

Figure 9.4 - Step 1: Define the Filter Criteria

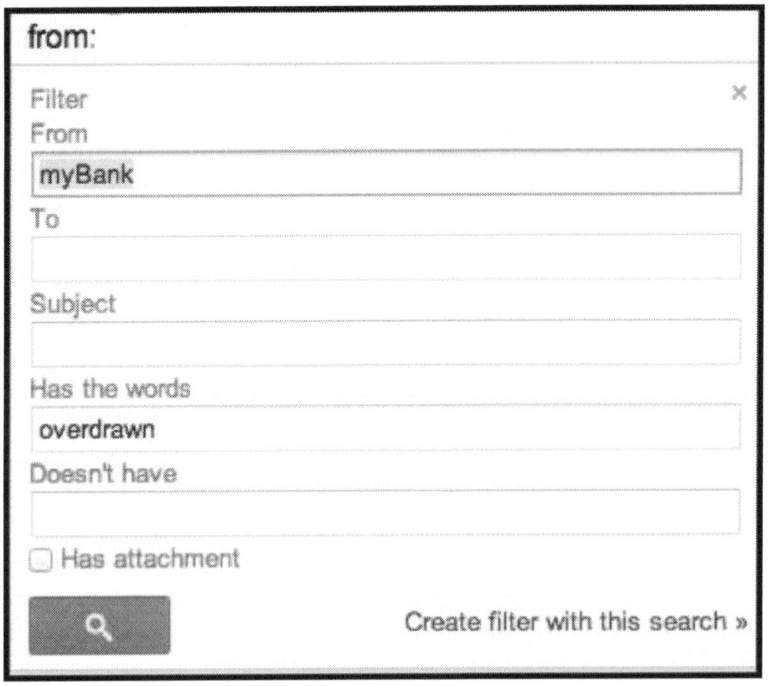

from:

Filter	×
From	
myBank	
To	
Subject	
Has the words	
overdrawn	
Doesn't have	
☐ Has attachment	
🔍	Create filter with this search »

In this example, I have set the filter criteria to be: message is from "myBank" and it contains the word "overdrawn". When you have specified all of the desired criteria, click "Create filter with this search". This will take you to the "Action" part of the filter as illustrated in Figure 9.5:

Figure 9.5 – Step 2: Specify What Actions to Apply to Selected Messages

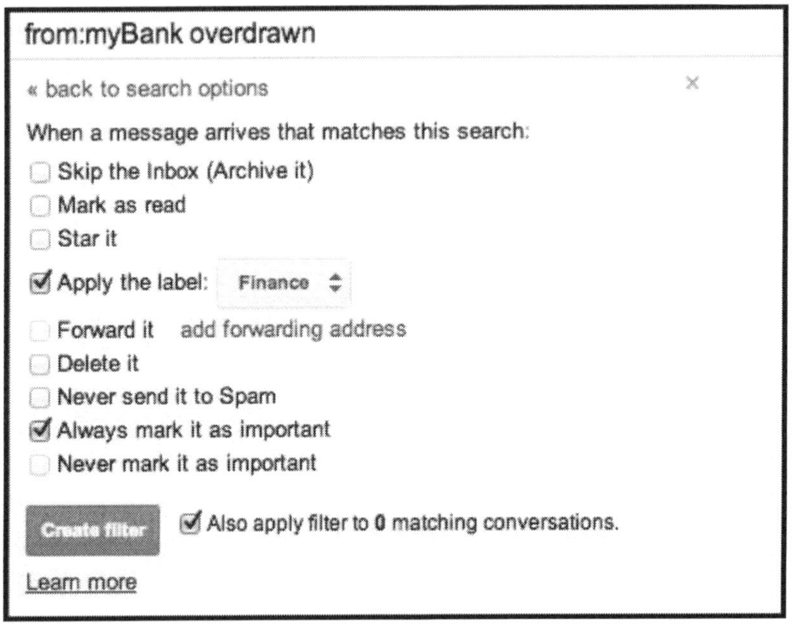

from:myBank overdrawn

« back to search options   ×

When a message arrives that matches this search:

☐ Skip the Inbox (Archive it)
☐ Mark as read
☐ Star it

☑ Apply the label: Finance ↕

☐ Forward it   add forwarding address
☐ Delete it
☐ Never send it to Spam
☑ Always mark it as important
☐ Never mark it as important

Create filter   ☑ Also apply filter to **0** matching conversations.

Learn more

In Figure 9.5 I have chosen the actions: Apply the "Finance" label and mark the message as Important. This filter will be applied to the message you started out with, and it will also be applied to any new incoming messages, but there may already be other messages in your Inbox that meet these filter criteria. So, I always check the box "Also Apply Filter to …". In this case there aren't any, but in general there may already be several messages in your Inbox. It is often the arrival of message after message that triggers the thought "Maybe I should Create a Filter". When you're all done, click "Create Filter".

9.3 - Gmail Settings

There are dozens of settings for Gmail. You access them by clicking on the "Gear Icon" in the upper right corner of the Gmail window and selecting "Settings" from the drop-down menu that appears. There are tabs across the top of the Settings window to select the type of settings you want to specify. I will touch on only a few of the more useful settings. The Tabs are:

General:

"Conversation View" - You can turn it on or off.

"Stars" - Select colors

"Signature" - create a signature for your outgoing messages

"Vacation Responder" - Automatically reply to messages you receive while on vacation

Labels:

Create, Edit, and Organize labels

Inbox:

Select the Inbox style you prefer

Accounts and Import:

Import mail and contacts from other email accounts

Import messages from POP accounts

Buy more space on Google servers

Filters:

Edit or Delete filters

Forwarding and POP/IMAP:

Set up mail forwarding

Set up POP Download

Set up IMAP Access

Chat:

Set up Chat

Web Clips:

Due to low interest, Google has removed customization

Labs:

A whole bunch of new stuff that Google is experimenting with

Offline:

You can install Gmail Offline to allow you to read and reply while offline

Themes:

Different appearances for the Gmail window

9.4 - Setting Up Gmail to Collect Mail from Your Other Accounts

If you already have an email account with some other provider, you can have Gmail collect mail sent to that account so that it will appear in your Gmail account. There are three ways to arrange for this to happen:

9.4.1 - Forwarding Mail from Your Old Account:

If your old email provider supports mail forwarding, you can arrange it so that any mail sent to your old account is forwarded to your Gmail account. You will have to contact your old email provider to find out if they support mail forwarding and, if they do, how to implement it. This will only forward messages that arrive in the future. All of your old messages will stay in your old account.

9.4.2 - Importing Mail and Contacts from Your Old Account:

If you have a lot of contacts and email messages stored in your old account and you would like to transfer them to your Gmail account, that may be possible depending upon who provides your old email service. Accounts with Yahoo!, Hotmail, and AOL do provide this service. Ironically Gmail does not. If your old account is with a different provider, you can check to see if they provide this service. To check, start by going here:

https://support.google.com/mail/bin/answer.py?hl=en&answer=164640&rd=1

Just a short distance down the page that opens you will see "**Click here to see which email providers are supported**". Click on that and a long list of providers will appear. If your provider isn't on the list, you can skip to the next section. If your provider is on the list, you should note that this is only a temporary process, it doesn't establish a permanent link between your old account and your Gmail account. You can have messages sent to your old account forwarded to your Gmail account for 30 days, but after that there will be no link between your accounts. Also note that this only imports messages you have received, not ones you have sent. To establish a permanent link between accounts, use "Mail Fetcher" as discussed in the next section.

To import messages and contacts from your old account:
- Open a Gmail window
- Click the "Gear" icon in the upper right corner

• Select "Settings" from the drop-down menu that appears
• Click on the "Accounts and Import" tab
• Click on "Import Mail and Contacts" (the blue one, not the title of the section which is black text)
• This will open a pane where you will sign-in to your other email account.
• Follow the subsequent steps.

When you finish, the import process will begin and a notice will appear in the "Import Mail and Contacts" section informing you of progress. Importing your old mail and contacts could take hours or days depending upon how much stuff you have accumulated.

9.4.3 - Fetching Mail from Your Other Accounts:

Gmail provides a facility called "Mail Fetcher" that can collect your old and new email messages from up to five other email accounts. These can be other Gmail accounts or accounts with other providers. Mail Fetcher can only fetch email from POP3 (Post Office Protocol) mail accounts. If you will be collecting messages from another email account, that account must have POP3 access enabled. You may have to contact your other email provider to see if they offer POP3 access and how to set it up on their end.

One of the nice things about Mail Fetcher is that it checks your other accounts for new mail on a more or less regular schedule so that, when you launch Gmail, your messages from other accounts will already be there. Mail Fetcher establishes a permanent link between accounts so that mail sent to your other account will continue to appear in your Gmail account indefinitely.

If you like, you can set up a Gmail filter to label messages fetched from other accounts with the name of that account so you can identify which message was sent to which account. First, create a Label with the name "myOldAccount" - of course you will use the actual name of your old account. Then set up a Filter with the criterion "To: myOldAccount" and action "Apply Label: myOldAccount". Now you will be able to recognize which messages came from which accounts, and you will also be able to see all messages from a particular account by clicking on the name of that account in the left sidebar. Refer back to section 9.2 for details about Labels and Filters.

To set up Mail Fetcher, follow these steps:

• With a Gmail window open, click the "Gear" icon and select "Settings"
• Click the "Accounts and Import" tab
• In the "Check Mail from Other Accounts" section, click "Add a POP3 Mail Account You Own"

That will open a pane where you will enter the address of the email account you want to fetch mail from. Click "Next Step" and continue to follow the steps for setting up Fetching from that account.

One decision you will have to make when setting up mail Fetching is whether to leave Fetched messages on the other account server. It is a good idea to leave messages on the server in case you want to access them from that or another account for some reason. In some cases the other account provider may delete Fetched messages even though you have chosen to leave them. This is an issue you will have to discuss with the other account provider.

Starting in December 2012, Gmail always uses SSL (encrypted) communications while sending, receiving, or Fetching email. If the provider of the account you want to Fetch mail from does not support SSL, your attempt to set up mail Fetching with that provider will fail. You can disable using SSL for an account, but that means that your user name and password will be sent un-encrypted over the internet. This is not good!

When you have finished setting up mail Fetching, you will see in the "Check Mail from Other Accounts" section a list of the accounts from which Gmail is Fetching mail. This list will also tell you when the last Fetch was performed. You can also edit or delete an account in this section.

9.4.4 - Sending Mail As:

While you're on the Gmail "Settings" page, just above the "Check Mail from Other Accounts" section you have been working in, is another section that you might find useful. This section is named "Send Mail As:". These settings allow you to set up and choose which accounts it will appear that your outgoing messages were sent from. In reality they will be sent from your Gmail account, but you can have it appear to the recipient that it was sent from one of the other accounts you own. Specifically, when you reply to an incoming message, you can choose whether that reply should appear to have come from your Gmail account or from the same account the original message was sent to.

I think it is useful to always have replies appear to come from my Gmail account regardless of which account the message I am replying to was sent to. In this way, my email contacts will eventually start using my Gmail account address.

9.5 - Working with the "New" Compose and Reply Experience

Google is currently "auditioning" a new format for the Compose and Reply windows in Gmail. By the time you read this, this "new" approach will probably be the standard. So, I will take a few pages to describe how this new approach works.

During the transition between the "Classical" and the "New" formats, you have the choice of which you want to use. Some features that are available in the Classical approach may not be functional yet in the New approach and you may want to switch back and forth between Classical and New.

9.5.1 - Switching between the Classical and the New Compose Experiences
---

Switching to the New Compose Experience:

If you are currently using the "Classical" Compose format, clicking on the "Compose" button will open a Compose window the top part of which will look like that shown in Figure 9.6.

Figure 9.6 - Switch to New from Classical

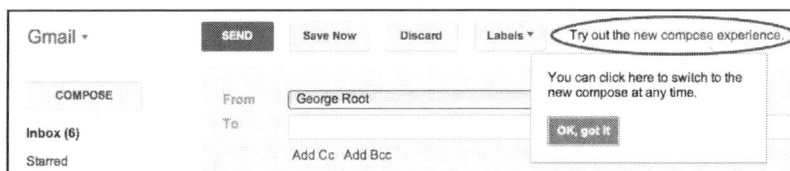

Clicking on the "Try Out the New Compose Experience" link will re-load your Gmail window using the new Compose features.

Switching Back to the Classical Compose Experience:

If you are currently using the "New" Compose format, clicking on the "Compose" button will open a Compose window the <u>bottom</u> part of which will look like that shown in Figure 9.7.

Figure 9.7 - Switch to Classical from New

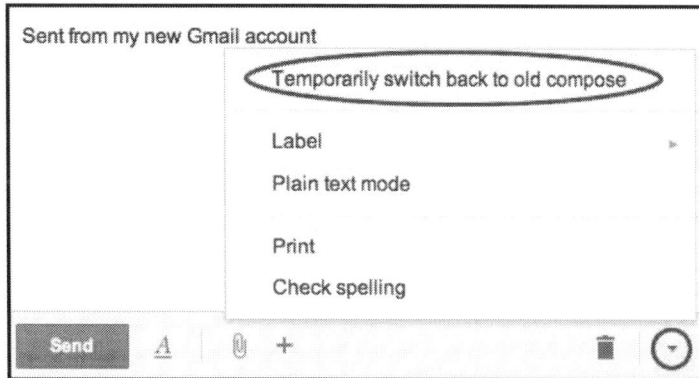

In the lower right corner of the new Compose window, there is a small downward pointing disclosure triangle circled in Figure 9.7. Clicking on this triangular icon will disclose a pop-up menu, also illustrated in Figure 9.7. Clicking on the top item, "Temporarily Switch Back to Old Compose", will do just that.

9.5.2 - Working With the New Compose Experience

When you click on the Compose button in the "New" format, a message window will open in the lower right corner of the Gmail window as illustrated in Figure 9.8.

Figure 9.8 - The New Compose Window

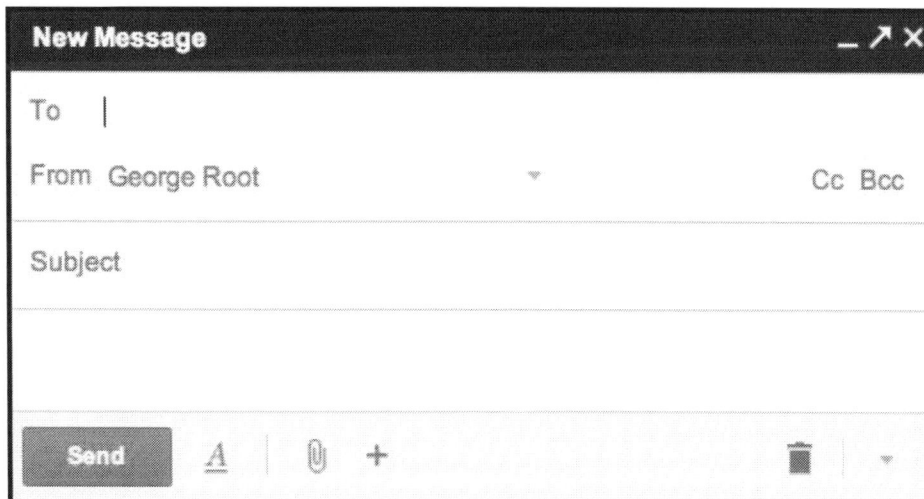

I have reduced the size of the actual message area in Figure 9.8 to save space, but it is pretty small in reality. I suspect that Google has analyzed the millions of email messages it sends each day and has found that most messages contain only a few lines of text. So a new Compose window has space for only a few lines of text. However, the window does grow automatically if you continue to type.

The new Compose and Reply windows are tethered to the lower right corner of the Gmail window which I find to be very annoying. I prefer to type somewhere near the center of my screen rather than down in the corner. Google does allow you to detach the message window so that you can resize it and move it around to where you want it to be.

To detach the Compose or Reply windows from the lower right corner, click on the upward pointing arrow icon shown in the upper right corner of Figure 9.8. It is called the "pop-out" icon and that's what it does - it pops out the Compose / Reply message window and places it somewhere near the center of the screen. You can now resize and move this window anywhere you choose.

There are two other icons in the upper right corner of the Compose / Reply window. The icon that looks like an "X" closes the window - it removes the window from the screen. However, if you have started composing your message, what you have done so far has already been saved in the "Drafts" mailbox. You can retrieve this Draft and continue to work on it by clicking on the "Drafts" mailbox in the left sidebar and then clicking on the message you want to complete.

The other icon in the upper right corner of the Compose / Reply window looks like the "_", underscore character. Clicking this icon will minimize the message window and store it at the bottom of the window as illustrated in Figure 9.9. You can retrieve the full size window by clicking anywhere on this minimized window icon.

Figure 9.9 - A "Minimized" Message Window Looks Like This

Along the bottom of the new Compose / Reply message window is a row of icons that looks like this:

Figure 9.10 - The Row of Icons at the Bottom of the Message Window

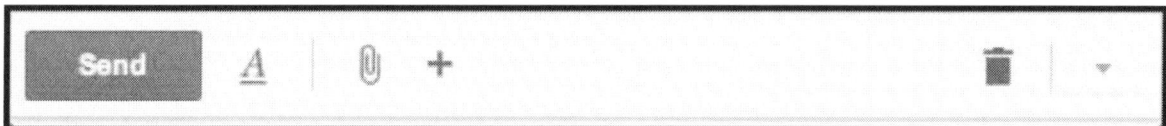

There are a lot of powerful features and capabilities hidden in this seemingly simple icon bar. The first icon that looks like an underlined italic "A" hides the formatting options that can be applied to the text in your message. Clicking on this icon will reveal another row of icons as illustrated in Figure 9.11.

Figure 9.11 - The Row of Text Formatting Icons

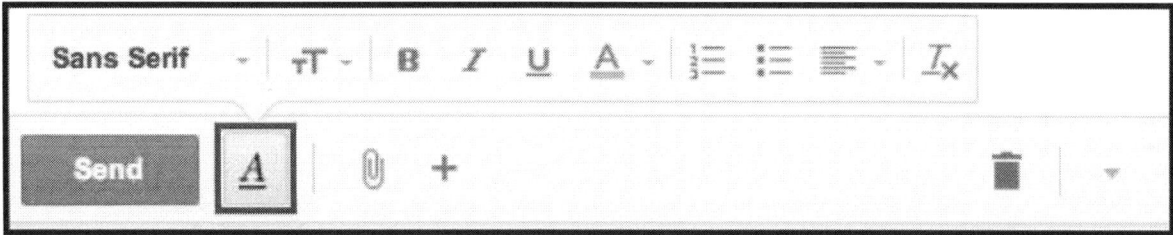

The first icon that appears in the row above the underlined italic "A" icon - the one that says "Sans Serif" in Figure 9.11 - allows you a small choice of fonts to use for your message. This selection is illustrated in Figure 9.12. To reach this list of fonts, you first click on the "Italic A" icon and then on the icon labeled "Sans Serif" in Figure 9.11 or 9.12.

Figure 9.12 - You Can Select a Font for Your Message from a Small Collection

The next icon in the formatting bar illustrated in Figure 9.11 - the one that looks like a small and large letter "T" - allows you to choose a font size for text in your message. This is illustrated in Figure 9.13 on the following page. The choices are only "Small", "Normal", "Large", and "Huge", but those are adequate for an email message. People with poor eyesight will really appreciate your using the "Large" or "Huge" font size.

The next three icons in Figure 9.11 that look like "**B** *I* U" apply the standard **Bold**, *Italic*, and Underlined style to any selected text in your message. Select the text you want to format and then click on one of these icons to apply that text style to the selected text.

Figure 9.13 - You Can Select a Font Size from a Small Collection of Sizes

The sixth icon in the formatting bar - the one that looks like an underlined "A" - is actually the text color chooser. Clicking on this icon reveals the color picker illustrated in Figure 9.14. You can select both the color of the text and also the color of the text background from this menu of colors. I'm sorry that this book is printed in black and white because Figure 9.14 is actually quite pretty with a nice selection of colors to choose from.

Figure 9.14 - You Can Select Colors for Text and for the Text Background

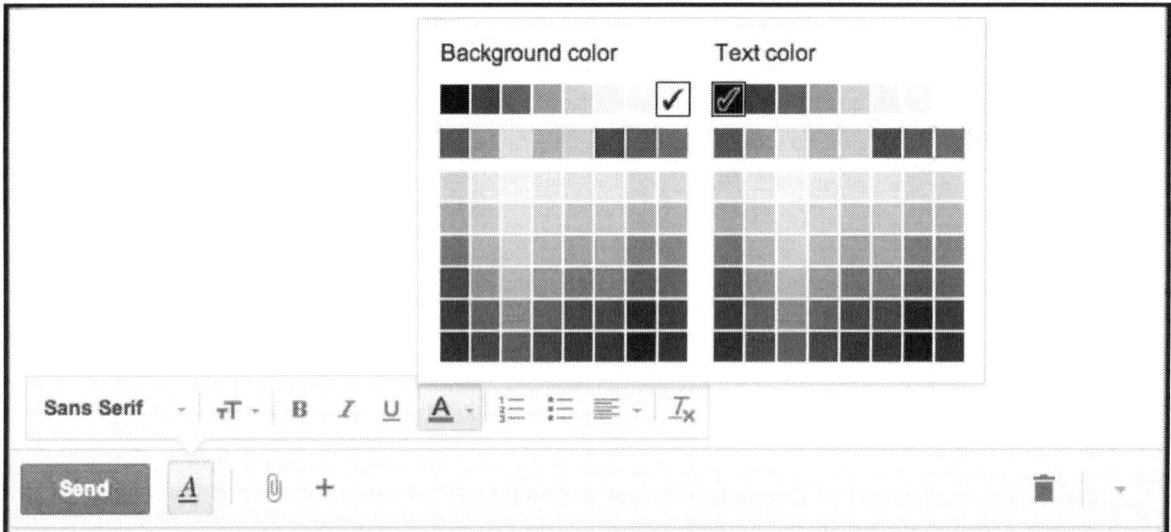

To the right of the Color Selector icon are two icons that look like numbered and bulleted lists. Clicking one of these icons will create a - you guessed it - numbered or bulleted list.

The next to last icon in the Formatting Bar - the one that looks like a set of long and short horizontal lines is actually quite powerful. Clicking on this icon reveals another formatting menu as illustrated in Figure 9.15.

Figure 9.15 - This Icon Reveals Six Alignment and Indentation Options

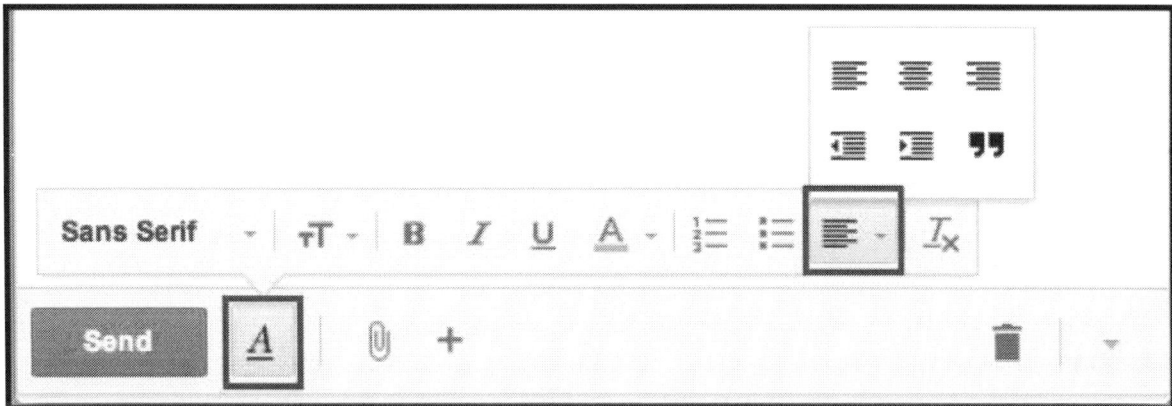

Of the six formatting options revealed by clicking on the two outlined icons in Figure 9.15, the top three are the standard "Left Justified", "Center Justified", and "Right Justified" options. The bottom row of three icons control how "Quoted Text" looks. "Quoted Text" and the function of these three icons is discussed in section 9.5.3.

But, before we move on to discussing Quoted Text, we haven't finished yet with the row of icons along the bottom edge of the "New" Compose / Reply window that is illustrated in Figure 9.10. You can also see this row of icons at the bottom of Figure 9.15 just above.

The next icon in the row at the bottom of a Compose / Reply window looks like a paperclip. This is a pretty standard icon for adding an attachment to your message and that's what this Paperclip does.

Figure 9.16 - The "Paperclip" Icon Allows You to Insert or Attach Something to Your Message

If you simply click on the Paperclip icon, that opens the file system on the computer you are using. If you're using a Chromebook, the Chromebook file system opens allowing you to choose a file from your "Drive" folder or your "Downloads" folder. If you are running the Chrome Browser on your personal computer, clicking on the Paperclip will open the file system on your computer. You can then select a file from your computer to attach to the Compose or Reply message.

However, if you don't actually click on the Paperclip icon, but rather just hover the cursor over it, that opens a row of icons to the right of the Paperclip as is illustrated in Figure 9.16. You can also click on the "+" symbol shown in Figure 9.15 to accomplish the same thing. This row of icons allows you to insert:

- A file from your Google Drive
- An image file from your computer
- A link to a website address (URL) or to an email address
- An "Emoticon" - those cute smiley faces
- A Calendar Invitation

The Trash Can icon discards the draft of the Compose / Reply message you are working on.

To the right of the Trash Can icon is a downward pointing disclosure triangle that, when clicked, opens a "More" pop-up menu. This menu is illustrated in Figure 9.7 where we used it to switch back to the "old" Compose / Reply format.

That's about it for the row of icons at the bottom of the "new" Compose / Reply window. We can now move on to:

9.5.3 - Working with Quoted Text in Replies

In the context of an email message, "Quoted Text" means text that originally appeared in a message you received and to which you are replying. It is often convenient to include portions of the original message in your reply in order to give your reply some context - just in case the person you are replying to has no idea what you are talking about. For example, in this snippet of text from a Reply message, the Reply "Yes it does!" makes a lot more sense when the quoted text "This is a test ..." is included.

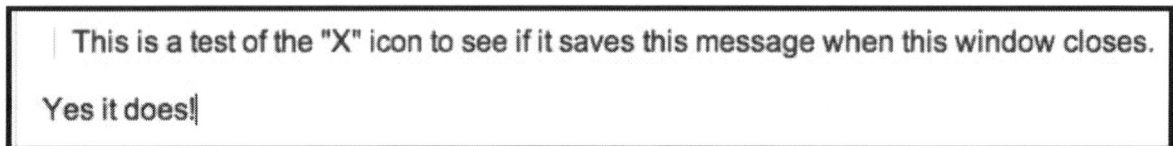

> This is a test of the "X" icon to see if it saves this message when this window closes.

Yes it does!

In an email reply, quoted text is indicated by a vertical line in the left margin and the quoted text itself is indented as illustrated in the figure above. Quoted text can also appear in Forwarded email messages. I'm sure we have all received messages that have been forwarded so many times that there are dozens of vertical lines along the left edge of the message. The number of vertical lines signifies the "quote level" of the quoted text - that is, how many times that text has been quoted before it reached you.

The two leftmost icons in the bottom row of three in Figure 9.15 decrease (the left icon) or increase (the right icon) the quote level of selected text. These two icons look as if they will reduce or increase the indentation of the text and that is exactly what they do.

The last icon in the bottom row - the one that looks like a giant quotation mark - makes plain text into quoted text, that is, it indents the text and places a vertical bar in the left margin.

There are a couple of ways to place text quoted from an original message into your reply. But first, we have to open a Reply window. Figure 9.17 is a message I sent to myself. This is the original message that I want to Reply to. In order to open the Reply message window, you can click on either of the "Reply" icons shown outlined in Figure 9.17 - they both do exactly the same thing. Figure 9.18 is an illustration of the Reply window that opens when you click on either Reply icon in an original Gmail message. Right now the Reply window is empty, just waiting for you to start typing your reply message. But, notice the three dots outlined in Figure 9.18. Clicking on this row of dots inserts the original message into your Reply as illustrated in Figure 9.19.

Figure 9.17 - You Can Start a Reply by Clicking Either of These Icons

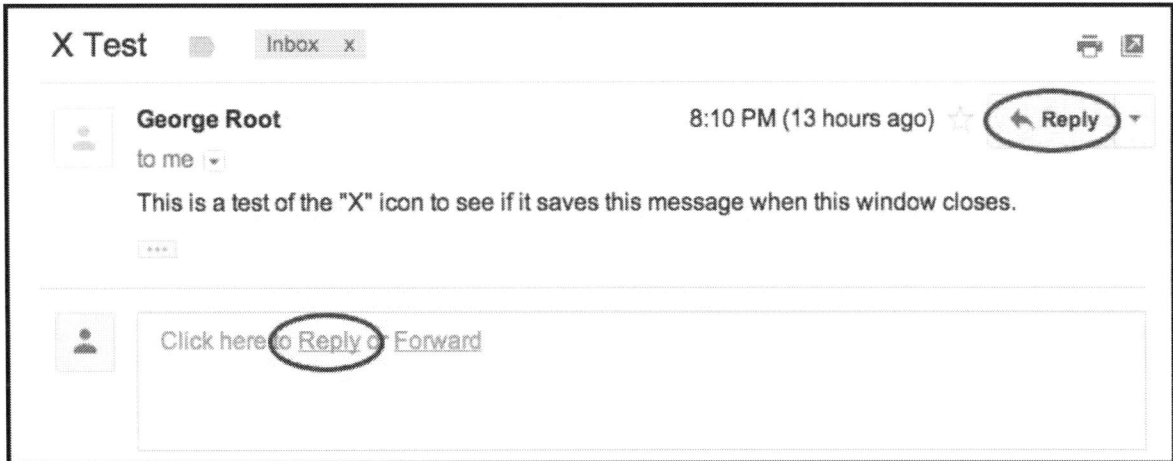

Figure 9.18 - Clicking on "Reply" in Figure 9.17 Opens a Reply Window

Figure 9.19 - Clicking on "…" in Figure 9.18 Quotes the Original Message in Your Reply

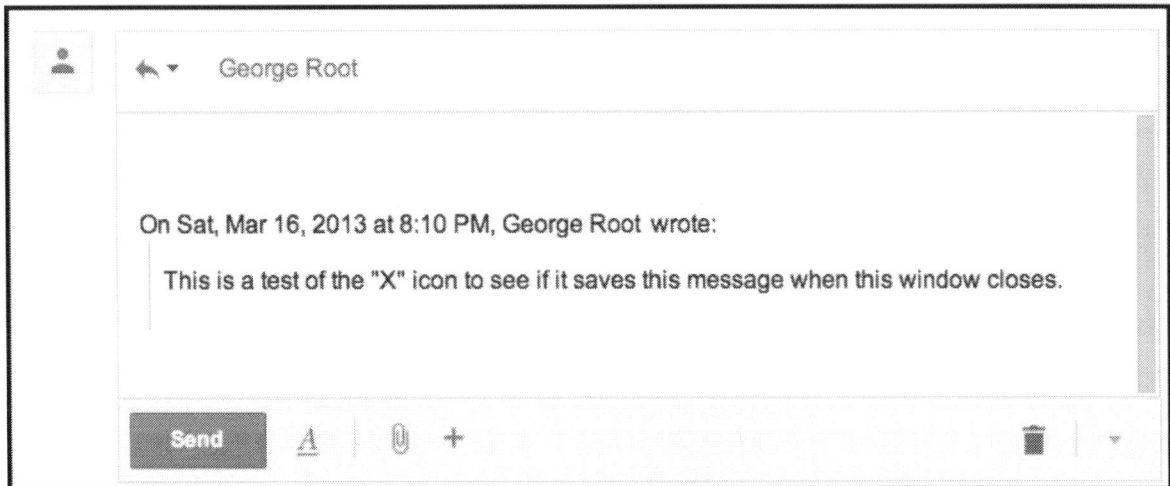

Cloud Computing with Google Chrome

You can edit the quoted text just as if you had typed it yourself. For example, the date stamp in Figure 9.19, "On Sat, Mar 16, 2013 …", is probably not important and it could be deleted.

If the original message is short, clicking on the "…" icon to quote the entire message in your reply is a viable option, but what if the original message were very long and you only wanted to reply to one part of it? There is another way to quote selected text from the original message. First, select and copy the text in the original message that you want to include in your reply. Then go to the Reply window and paste the copied text. It will appear as regular, that is unquoted, text. You could put quotation marks around it to indicate that it is quoted, but that's not the way email quoted text is displayed. To convert your pasted text into "true" quoted text, go back to Figure 9.15 and click on the big black quotation marks that are illustrated in the lower right corner of the pop-out menu. When you do this, the cursor has to be somewhere within the text you want to "quote". Clicking on this icon will indent the paragraph containing the cursor and will place a vertical line at the left margin.

But wait, there is yet another way to place quoted text into your reply. It is a shortcut of the method just described. In order to use this shortcut, you first have to "enable" it. The shortcut is just one of the many things that Google is experimenting with in the Google "Labs". When "enabled", this shortcut allows you to select some text from the original message. Then, when you click on Reply, that text will already be there and it will be quoted.

To enable the "Quote Selected Text" shortcut:

- Click on the Gear icon in the upper right corner of a Gmail window
- Select "Settings"
- Click on the "Labs" tab
- Scroll down and find the "Quote Selected Text" item
- Click on "Enable"
- Click on "Save Changes" at the bottom of the window!

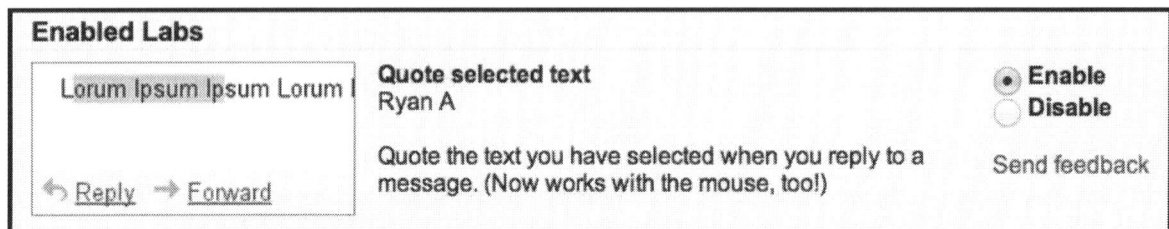

There are a lot of other things Google is experimenting with in the "Labs" tab. You might want to browse around while you're there. For example, I also enabled a "Mark as Unread" button.

106

9.6 - Working with Contacts

Your Contacts are managed as part of Gmail. There is no separate "Contacts" app. To get to your Contacts, you first open a Gmail window and then click on the downward pointing disclosure triangle just to the right of the "Gmail" banner near the upper left corner of the window. Then click on "Contacts".

Figure 9.20 - Contacts are Accessed via the Gmail Banner

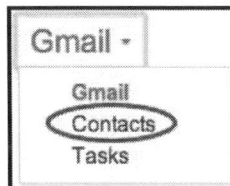

You can also get to your Contacts page by going here:

www.google.com/contacts

9.6.1 Adding Contacts

Contacts are automatically added to your Contact list whenever you Reply to, or Forward an email message to someone not already in your Contacts list. If you use Google+, adding a person to your "Circle" will also add that person to your Contacts list. If you find a message from someone you know in your Spam mailbox and you mark that message as "Not Spam", the Contact entry for that person will be updated so that future messages from that person will not be marked as Spam. You will find these automatically added Contacts in the "Other Contacts" group in the left sidebar of the Contacts window.

If you end up with a lot of automatically added Contacts that you really didn't want, you can turn off automatic Contacts as follows:

- Open a Gmail window
- Click on the Gear icon near the upper right corner of the window
- Select "Settings"
- In the "General" tab, find "Create Contacts for Auto-Complete"
- Choose "I'll Add Contacts Myself"

You can also add Contacts manually. Clicking on the big red "New Contact" button in the upper left corner of the Contacts window takes you to a page where you can enter information for your new contact. This is illustrated in Figure 9.21

Figure 9.21 - You Can Add Contacts by Clicking on "New Contact"

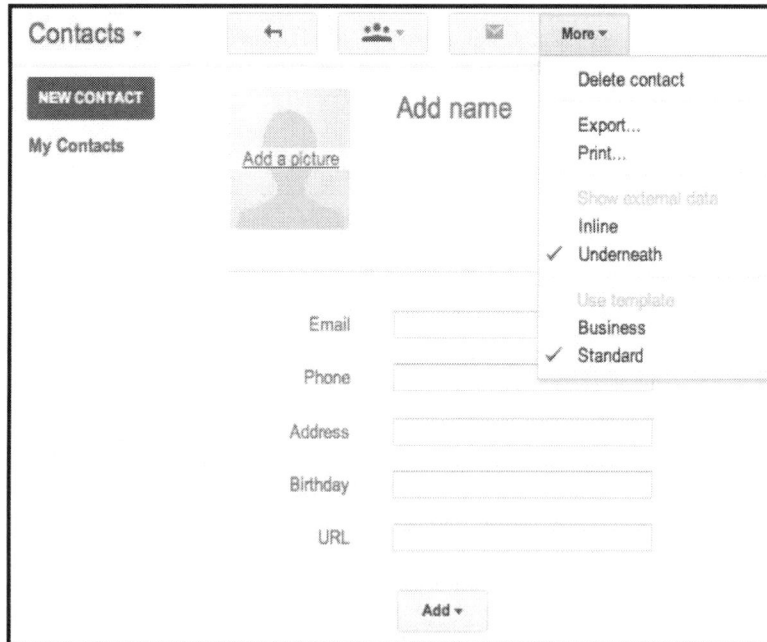

The icons along the top of the "New Contact" pane illustrated in Figure 9.21 are:

- The left pointing arrow takes you back to your Contacts list
- The "crown" icon adds this contact to a contact group. You can also create new contact groups here.
- The "envelope" icon starts an email message to this contact
- The "More" button drops down the menu illustrated in Figure 9.21

The "Add" button at the bottom of the page leads to a menu where you can add more fields to your Contact information - for example: title and company. You can also create your own custom fields here.

9.6.2 Importing Contacts from Other Apps

There are two ways that other apps export their contacts information: either as a CSV (Comma Separated Values) list, or as a vCard file.

Apps like Outlook, Outlook Express, Yahoo! Mail, Hotmail, and Eudora export their contact information as a CSV list. Apps like Outlook and Mac "Contacts" export their contact information in vCard format. Whichever format is used by your other contacts app, export the information for the contacts you want to transfer to Gmail. You will usually just select the contacts and then choose "Export" from a menu somewhere. Be sure to choose either "CSV" or "vCard" if given the choice. If you need help exporting Contacts from other email providers:

http://support.google.com/mail/bin/answer.py?hl=en&answer=12118&topic=1669027&ctx=topic

Once you have exported your Contacts from your other app, perform the following steps.

- Open a Gmail window
- Choose "Contacts" from the drop down menu illustrated in Figure 9.20
- From the "More" drop down menu illustrated in Figure 9.22 choose "Import"
- Click the "Choose File" button
- Select the file you exported and click "Import"

Figure 9.22 - You Can Import Contact Information from Other Apps

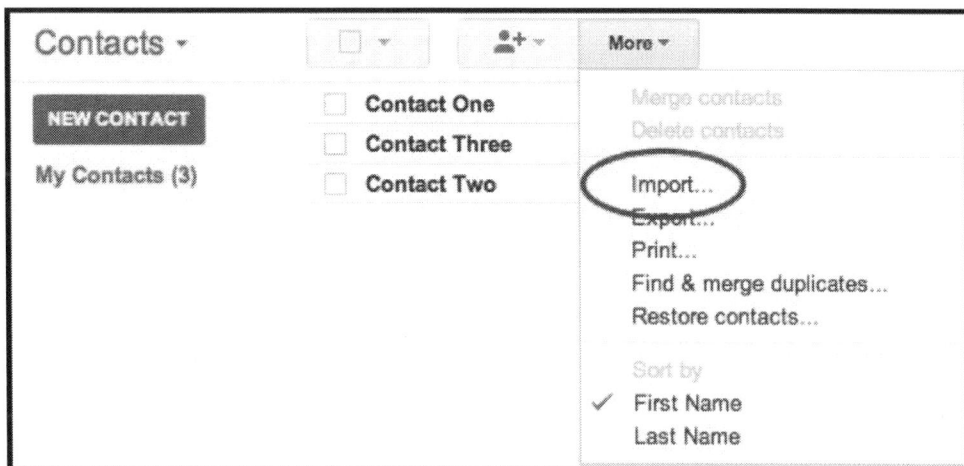

9.7 - Variations on Your Gmail Address

Sometimes, when you have to give your Gmail address to someone or some company, you would like to keep track of where that address goes. You give the address to Paul's Pizza and soon thereafter you start getting junk mail from Sam's Sandwiches. Did Paul sell your address to Sam? You can track your Gmail address by using "variations".

There are two types of variations that Gmail allows:

1) Add "Dots" to your address. For example, myAddress@gmail.com is, as far as Gmail is concerned, exactly the same as my.Add.ress@gmail.com. You can add as many "dots" (i.e. periods) to your Gmail user name as you like. Mail sent to the "dotted" address will still reach your InBox because Gmail ignores "dots". But you will see the dots and be able to tell where that address came from.

2) Add "+..." to your address. For example, myAddress+Paul@gmail.com is, as far as Gmail is concerned, exactly the same as myAddress@gmail.com. Gmail ignores anything after the "+". So, if your email message from Sam is addressed to myAddress+Paul@gmail.com you will know that Paul is the one who sold your address.

I think that this feature has limited utility, but if the situation arises where this would be useful, it is nice to know that it is there.

9.8 - Signing-Out of Your Gmail Session

If you are using your personal computer or Chrome Device at home, you might choose to stay signed-in to your Gmail account rather than having to sign-in each time you want to read your email. If you do want to sign-out, just click on the downward pointing disclosure triangle next to your email address near the top right corner of the Gmail window and click on the "Sign-Out" button.

But, what if you have used a public computer at the library or an Internet cafe to check your Gmail and you forgot to sign-out when you left? That's bad. But again, Google comes to the rescue. Open a Gmail window and scroll down to the bottom of the window. In the bottom right corner you will see a link "Details". Click on this and a pane will open listing recent activity on your account. There is a button near the top of this pane labeled "Sign Out of All Other Sessions". Click that!

10 - Using Google Groups

As useful as this book has been (at least I hope it has been), there are a lot of topics and questions I haven't covered. You can read more about any Google topic by searching out the Google Support Webpages on that topic. I have given several links to these pages as we have progressed through the book.

There is another valuable resource made available by Google where Chrome users can ask questions and discuss various topics. These are the discussion forums that are collectively known as Google Groups. There is at least one Google Group devoted to just about any topic you can think of. They are not just Google or Chrome related.

Google Groups are divided into two general categories: "Google Groups" which are devoted to any topic and "Google Product Forums" which cover specific Google products. This is probably a good place to look for help if you have a question or problem that others may have solved. You can reach the "Google Products Forums" main webpage at:

http://support.google.com/bin/static.py?hl=en&page=portal_groups.cs

Figure 10.1 - A Small Portion of the Google Product Forums Available

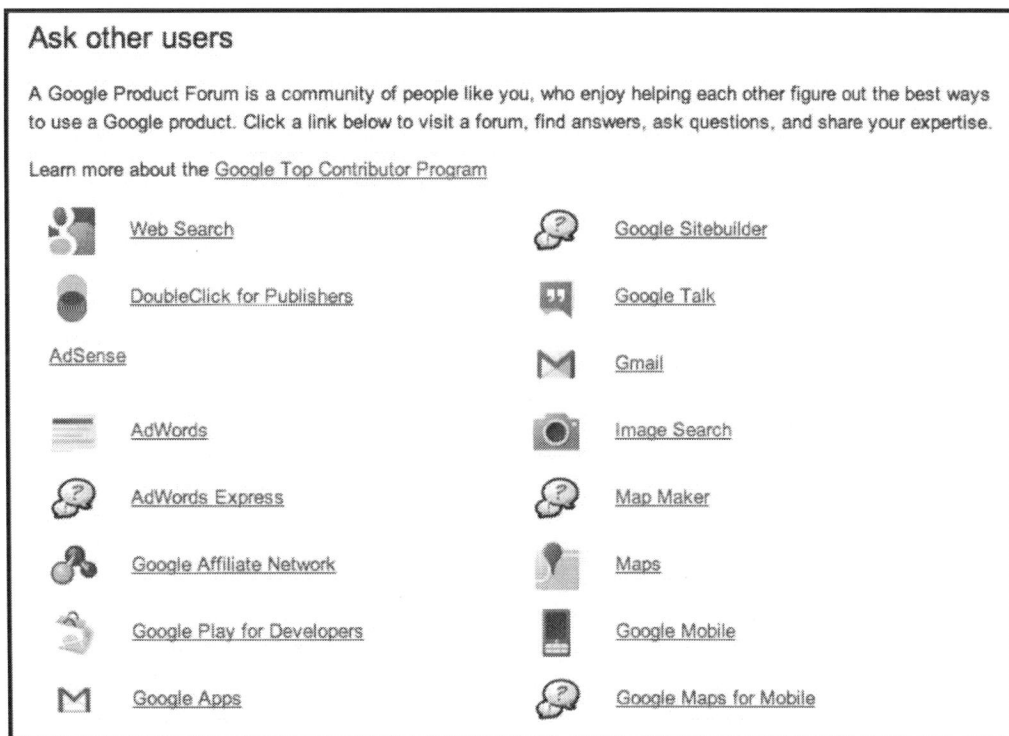

Ask other users

A Google Product Forum is a community of people like you, who enjoy helping each other figure out the best ways to use a Google product. Click a link below to visit a forum, find answers, ask questions, and share your expertise.

Learn more about the Google Top Contributor Program

Web Search	Google Sitebuilder
DoubleClick for Publishers	Google Talk
AdSense	Gmail
AdWords	Image Search
AdWords Express	Map Maker
Google Affiliate Network	Maps
Google Play for Developers	Google Mobile
Google Apps	Google Maps for Mobile

Figure 10.1 shows just a tiny portion of the long list of Google Product Forums that you can consult for answers to your questions. There are many more than I have shown here. As an example, there is a Google Product Support forum, shown in Figure 10.1, devoted to Gmail. Clicking on the link to this forum opens the page, a portion of which is shown in Figure 10.2.

Figure 10.2 - A Small Portion of the Google Product Forum for Gmail

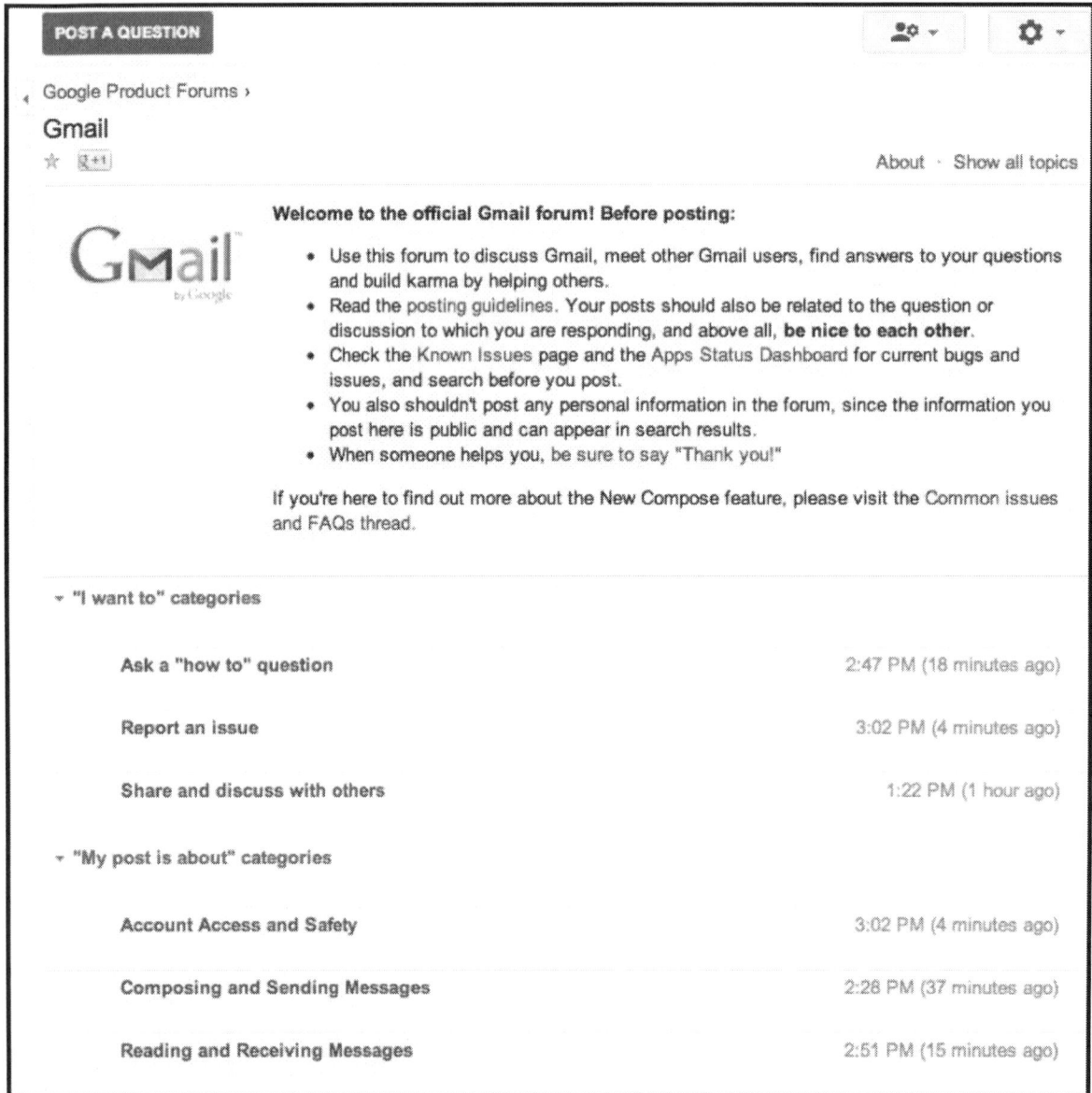

You can explore this and other "official" Google Support Forums by starting with the portal illustrated in Figure 10.1.

In addition to the "official" Google forums, there are also less formal groups where people with similar interests can discuss, ask questions, and provide answers. The portal to these discussion groups can be found here:

https://groups.google.com/forum/?fromgroups#!overview

Following this link will bring you to this webpage:

Figure 10.3 - The Start Page for Google Groups

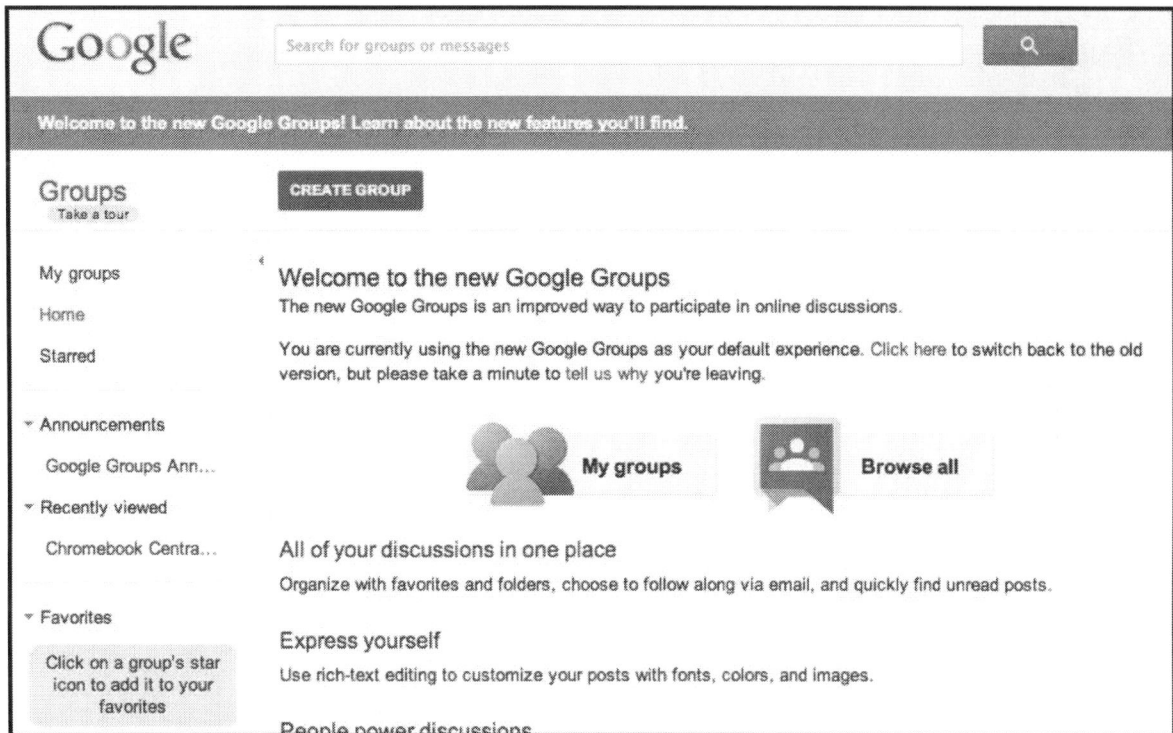

If you have already joined some groups, you can access them by clicking on the "My Groups" button. But, if you are just starting out, you can find groups that might interest you by clicking on the "Browse" button. Doing that will bring you to the webpage, a portion of which is shown in Figure 10.4 on the next page. This page lists very broad categories of topics. Start narrowing your search by clicking on one of these broad categories. In Figure 10.4 I have clicked on the "Computers" category shown outlined in red.

Clicking on "Computers" in Figure 10.4 narrows the range of topics to those shown in Figure 10.5, also on the next page. In this figure, I have clicked on the "Operating Systems" link which took me to the page illustrated in Figure 10.6 where I found a specific group devoted to discussions of "Chromebooks". Clicking on the name of that group in Figure 10.6 brought me to the actual Google Group illustrated in Figure 10.7. At this point you could join that group, read posts, or ask a question that other group members might be able to answer.

Once again, there's a lot more to learn about Google Groups, but this should be enough to get you started.

Figure 10.4 - Browse for Broad Categories of Topics

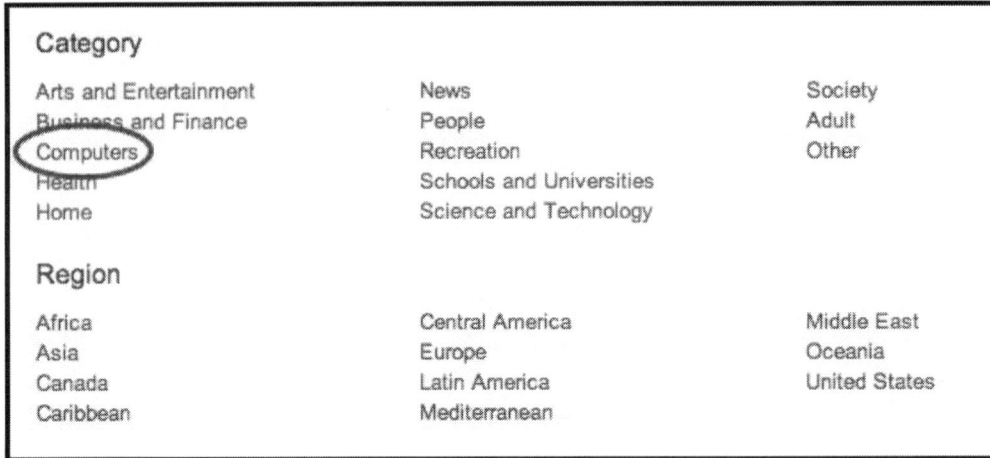

Category

Arts and Entertainment	News	Society
Business and Finance	People	Adult
Computers	Recreation	Other
Health	Schools and Universities	
Home	Science and Technology	

Region

Africa	Central America	Middle East
Asia	Europe	Oceania
Canada	Latin America	United States
Caribbean	Mediterranean	

Figure 10.5 - Narrow Your Search to More Specific Topics

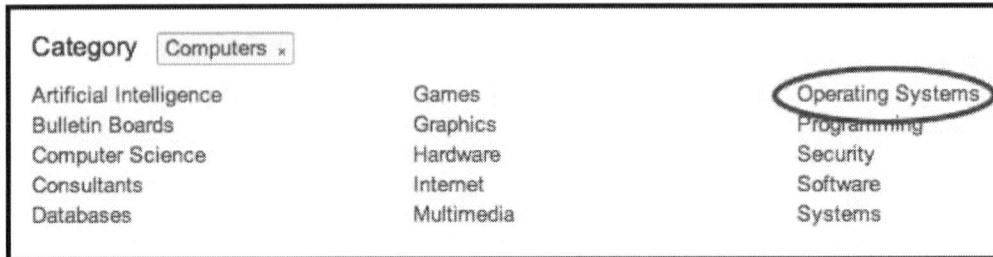

Category [Computers ×]

Artificial Intelligence	Games	Operating Systems
Bulletin Boards	Graphics	Programming
Computer Science	Hardware	Security
Consultants	Internet	Software
Databases	Multimedia	Systems

Figure 10.6 - Finally Find a Specific Google Group that Interests You

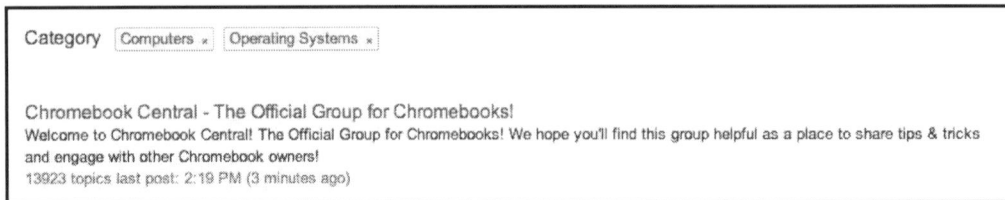

Category [Computers ×] [Operating Systems ×]

Chromebook Central - The Official Group for Chromebooks!
Welcome to Chromebook Central! The Official Group for Chromebooks! We hope you'll find this group helpful as a place to share tips & tricks and engage with other Chromebook owners!
13923 topics last post: 2:19 PM (3 minutes ago)

Figure 10.7 - The "Chromebook Central" Group Where the Discussions Occur

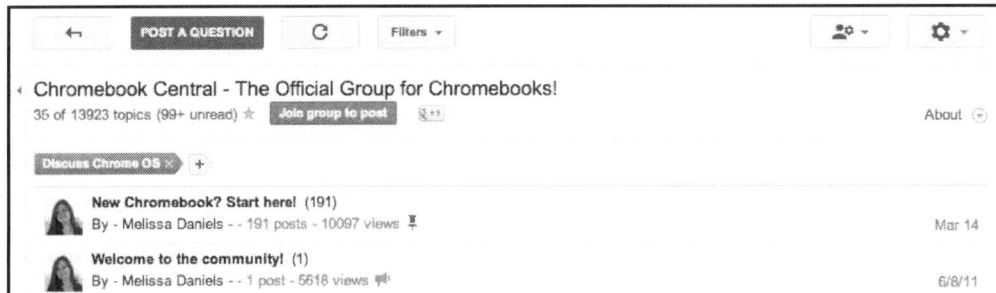

Chromebook Central - The Official Group for Chromebooks!
35 of 13923 topics (99+ unread) Join group to post   About

Discuss Chrome OS × +

New Chromebook? Start here! (191)
By - Melissa Daniels - - 191 posts - 10097 views   Mar 14

Welcome to the community! (1)
By - Melissa Daniels - - 1 post - 5618 views   6/8/11

11 - Things to Come

As I'm writing this, Google has just released Chrome stable version 25 and beta version 26 with some new capabilities that will begin showing up in Chrome apps soon. Chrome 25 includes OS support for speech recognition - the ability to talk to apps and have them recognize what you said. It still remains for app developers to make use of this capability by writing apps that accept spoken input. Expect to see these apps in the near future. Google search already has speech recognition capability so you can try it out for yourself right now. Wherever you see a small microphone icon, for example, at the right end of a Google search box, just click on that icon and start talking.

Google has also purchased "QuickOffice" with plans to integrate it into Google Drive. This will give Chrome users the ability to work directly with Microsoft Office files without having to convert them into Google Docs formats.

Google has announced that as of July 1, 2013, it will no longer provide the Google Reader app. This was a useful rss feed reader. There are several alternatives in the Chrome Web Store. "Feedly" has announced that it intends to offer the services previously provided by Reader.

Google is also expanding the availability of "Google Now", previously an Android mobile app, to the Chrome browser and Chrome OS. This is Google's effort to provide useful, timely, and personalized information without the user having to ask for it. For example, the user might get a notification in the morning telling about the day's weather, or the current driving time to work. This is one example of what appears to be Google's plans to merge the Chrome and Android operating systems.

In addition to adding functional capabilities to Chrome, Google also patched some 22 security risks. Among these it disabled silent extension installations on Windows PCs. This eliminated a problem where, if you were installing an extension that you approved, you might also get some added extensions that you knew nothing about. Starting with version 25, you must approve the installation of every extension and app.

The future of Chrome looks bright!

That's it for this book. I hope you found something useful in it. If you have any feedback, if you have found any of my mistakes, or if you would like me to add something in a future update, please let me know. You can send me email at:

ChromeBookFeedback@gmail.com

Printed in Great Britain
by Amazon.co.uk, Ltd.,
Marston Gate.